Bored In The Eighties

A Real Teenage Diary

Volumes 1 & 2

MARK HIGHWATER

The Silvinity Press

Copyright © 2025 Mark Highwater

First published in 2025 by The Silvinity Press.

All rights reserved.

No part of this book may be reproduced, stored in a retrieval system, or transmitted in any form or by any means, electronic, mechanical, photocopying, recording, or otherwise, without the prior written permission of the copyright holder.

ISBN: 9798306338293

www.thesilvinitypress.uk

INTRODUCTION

In October 1982, Sue Townsend first published 'The Secret Diary of Adrian Mole, Aged 13¾'. It was a best-seller, and soon spawned a sequel, 'The Growing Pains of Adrian Mole' in August 1984.

Like countless other teenage boys, I was totally engrossed in the books. Despite being written by a woman in her mid-thirties, the character of Adrian Mole seemed to perfectly capture the awkwardness and bewilderment we all felt, growing up in a dull world that we struggled to understand. Adrian however, recounted his life in a way that provided high entertainment value, because of course – it was fiction. Our lives weren't really like that. We just wished that they were.

So maybe it was simply a desperate attempt at transference that led kids like me to start our own diaries. If we wrote it all down, would the curtain fall and reveal hitherto unnoticed layers of intrigue, jeopardy, comedy and drama? I think you can guess the answer to that question from the title of this book.

Unlike the Mole diaries, I rarely mention my parents (if anything this was Townsend's tell – I don't believe any 13 year old paid that much attention to their parents' lives!), and whereas Adrian's cast of school friends is small, mine is sprawling, with most only making brief appearances. Where he has enemies, I have none, and where he expresses his hopes and dreams, my only aspiration seems to be seeing Samantha Fox in stages of undress. The word "bored" appears dozens of times.

Sue Townsend perfected a wonderful literary and comedic device - the gap between Adrian's perception and the reality that we could all see between the lines. This being a 'real-life diary', there is no such deliberate framing of the story. In fact, I made a conscious decision to reproduce the diary entries verbatim, with the only redactions being those which maintained the privacy of others. There seemed little point in trying to rewrite my own personal history. Therefore the only humour to be found is in the accidentally pathos-laden text which was set out before me. Some of it really was an excruciating read. So if the book doesn't work for you as a historical document of teenage 1980s, then if nothing else, you get to witness a grown man drowning in his own embarrassment.

* * *

I began to write these diaries over forty years ago, and since then they have remained in a locked briefcase in my attic.

In 1995, when I bought my first house, I was too attached to my childhood to throw them away, but too afeared and uncomfortable to still have them lying around. I just safely stored them in the eaves and promptly forgot about them.

It wasn't until recent events led me to try and clear space in the attic that I rediscovered the briefcase and dared to look at what the teenage me had left behind.

What I found was a set of eight, identical red A5 Silvine notebooks, starting on January 1st 1985, when I had just turned 14, and ending on 14th August 1990 aged 19. They were falling apart and considerably worse for wear from conditions they'd endured in the roof space for the past four decades. Having been written in fountain pen also didn't help, as the ink was beginning to fade. My instinct to immediately destroy them was quickly over-ruled by my curiosity to read a few entries for old times' sake.

An hour later and I was still absorbed in the contents. Transported back to my youth. Trying to decipher my bloody awful handwriting. Cringing. Laughing. Connecting dots. Understanding things about my childhood through the prism of being a parent to two boys of my own. Recognising the frustrations I sometimes feel as a Dad, are the same ones I invoked in my own Father. Remembering that we were all kids once.

I realised there was no way I could bring myself to bin them, but also, that if I didn't do something to preserve them, they might soon be lost forever.

So, at first, I began to type them out, purely for my own benefit. However, it didn't take long before it started to feel like I was dealing with a real historical artefact. A document of a world that no longer existed—neither physically nor emotionally. If the diaries felt like that now, how would they read in another forty years (in other words, when I am dead and I can no longer explain to my be-jetpacked, Mars-dwelling descendants what any of my rambling nonsense meant)?

Hence my efforts here to, not just transcribe, but also to explain a lot of what was (and more importantly *wasn't*) going on.

One thing I found is that time and memory are strange beasts. There are incidents I remember vividly (but which I don't diarise in detail) and other times there are lengthy explanations of things that happened which I genuinely can't remember (even after reading about them in my own hand). My marginalia against most entries attempts to make sense of all of this.

* * *

A quick explainer of the format. Although the book contains Volumes 1 & 2 of the Silvine diaries, it is actually split into 3 parts.

In amongst the contents of the briefcase, I unexpectedly found a handful of pages, ripped from a school exercise book, that actually contained my first aborted attempt at writing a diary. These pages consisted of entries which covered a week in August 1984 when I was still 13 (and, crucially I had just read the second, brand new, Adrian Mole book on holiday), and then a final interim entry at the end of November 1984 where I filled in a few gaps and expressed my intent to start again in a proper notebook. These remnants form '*The Torn Out Pages*' opening section.

The remaining two sections cover Volumes 1 and 2 of the diaries (as pictured on the front cover.)

Volume 1 starts with good intentions and I write an entry every day for four months. Volume 2 continues that streak and I manage another month or so of daily entries before things become more sporadic. By the time my journaling in Volume 2 returns to some semblance of regularity, I have left school and I'm 17 years old, attending Sixth-Form College.

At the back of each notebook were a series of "Personal Stats" at random dated intervals. These are inserted into their logical place within the narrative.

Of the remaining Volumes, still to be transcribed, the next 5 have several updates per week and each one covers a 4 month time period. The final Volume is more infrequent and concludes several pages before the end of the notebook, just a few months before my teenage years drew to a close. I never kept a diary again.

THE TORN OUT PAGES

(August 13th 1984 to December 10th 1984)

Monday, August 13th, 1984

Called for Evs this morning.

We watched Laurel & Hardy films on TV. Funny.

Saw Louise this afternoon and she looked really fit in her yellow and white string vest dress. If only she wasn't going out with that big nosed git Wilko. I hate him. Just as much as I love Louise.

Me and Evs spent the afternoon walking around the estate with her and her Sister. Her Sister had her hair done at the place next to the Corner Shop.

Evs scrounged loads of food off me, and then we got shouted at by a bloke for genie-ing a matchbox.

Not sure if this is still a thing, but to "genie" a matchbox, meant to light one match and then use that lit match to set fire to the whole pack. It was a great way to have 5 seconds of fun for the sake of a 5p box of matches. And lose your eyebrows sometimes.

Louise was a girl in my class that I fancied like mad. We had one slow dance (George Michael's 'Careless Whisper) at the school end-of-term disco in July. I got an erection and had to disguise the fact by dancing like I'd dislocated my hips. That was the extent of our relationship.

Tuesday, August 14th, 1984

Didn't do a lot today. Evs couldn't come out because he had to do some stupid ironing for his Mum.

I changed my bank account to 'Young Savers'. Totally don't know why. My Mum just said I should.

My boring Scottish Godmother came today with her 2 pain in the arse brat kids. I kept them happy by taking them on the park. We climbed under some hedges into the gardens of the big private houses that back on to the park.

Didn't see Louise at all today. I have withdrawal complaints.

Apparently the big-nose Wilko wants to fight me. He reckons he's been going out with Louise since Easter. That's almost 4 months. I think someone told him about the school disco. If she was going out with him, why did she agree to dance with me anyway?

Evs better come out tomorrow and I hope that I definitely see Louise.

Evs was a lovely lad and a great friend. His Dad wasn't around and he was only child. Just him and his Mum. It's fair to say he was quite a lot more mature than I was. He'd had to be. The idea that he did the ironing was clearly horrifying to me.

Wednesday, August 15th, 1984

Today was even more boring than yesterday! Called for Evs in the morning and he was having a massive argument with his Mum, and as I waited at the door I heard his Mum say *"Do you want me to tell him to get stuffed?"*. Evs said *"yeah"*

I don't think he was in a very good mood at that precise moment. His Mum then answered the door and said he was *"too busy"*. She is a fibber!

I did catch a brief glimpse of my darling Louise. She was in their brown Mini driving down the street into town. I had rung her house earlier but the line was engaged. Probably with that twat Wilko.

If I don't see her tomorrow, I might die.

If Evs doesn't come round, I'll be really angry.

Oh no! Disaster! I've just found out that we have to go and visit Nanna tomorrow. No Louise for another day. I might as well end it all now.

I'm preparing for a complete day of boredom tomorrow. It always is there.

It is still an immutable fact of life that, when you are 14, being made to visit your Grandparents is simply the WORST thing ever. But Jesus, what I wouldn't give to spend another couple of hours with them now.

Thursday, August 16th, 1984

Today was not quite as boring as I expected. We arrived in the morning to find my Uncle Clarence staying with Nanna & Grandad. Then he went home and we had dinner (sandwiches).

My Mum went to fetch my other Nanna who is recovering from a cataract operation on her eye.

We looked through loads of old photos of Nanna & Grandad when they were young. Nanna gave me a photo of Grandad when he was in the Home Guard (like Dad's Army!)

She also gave me the first part of 'Albert & The Lion' written by her Mum (my Great-Grandma that I never met). She played me the record of it and then gave it me to bring home so I can learn it. It is a 78rpm!

3 days now without seeing Louise! I'll have to see her tomorrow, so Evs better come out.

The days of this week seem to get more boring each day. Tomorrow cannot be worse than today.

Annoyingly I don't seem to be able to find this photo, but I do still have the record, and I can indeed recite (most of) it from memory.

Friday, August 17th, 1984

I'm in luck. Today was only semi-boring.

Evs had to paint a door in the morning and in the afternoon we went swimming with the Holiday Club people. We went in the Family Pool and it was semi-boring. We had an interesting conversation with the swimming man about Holiday Club and how much Evs was acting like a wally.

It has now been 4 days without seeing Louise. It has probably given her enough time to see that twat Wilko without having her eye poked out by his nose.

Evs scrounged some more money off me at the Baths. He better pay me back.

Bought a Mr Freeze ice pop this morning for 4p.

Performing all normal bodily functions i.e. farting, pissing, breathing in and out etc. Boring.

Evs says he is definitely coming out tomorrow. Not sure whether I believe him or not.

Oh well. Time for bed said Zebedee. Exact time 11:28pm

Zzzzzzz

See what I mean about Evs being grown up? "Painting a door"??

Saturday, August 18th, 1984

Dear Diary,

Sorry about falling asleep last night. 1000 apologies.

Lots of love,

Me

Xxxx

Pretty decent day today. Mainly because I briefly saw my beloved, Louise, although I didn't speak to her. She was with Jayne all afternoon.

My Aunty Marion and Nanna came to visit for tea (boring).

Evs gave me a backy on his bike and I completely crapped myself. Then he fell off his bike and hit his head. I wonder if he has delayed concussion yet? Evs are you receiving me? Ommmm! Ommmm! Hmm – no answer. Must be unconscious.

It's 11:57pm. It was Donington Monsters Of Rock today. Wish I'd been there. Knackered now. Night all.

AC/DC headlined Donington in 1984 and I was a big fan, but having since been to Monsters Of Rock (now Download) as an adult, I think it's fair to say that I wouldn't have survived it long as a 13 year old.

Sunday, August 19th, 1984

V. Crap day today. Did sweet FA. Had no cash and did not see mon cheri Louise. We sat around at the bottom of her road in the hope that she might come out, and we were bored so throwing stones at the street sign. Some bloke came and told us to 'piss off'! Evs gave him a load of lip in return.

Then a kid came up to us and threatened us, but Evs stood up to him (my hero!). It was boiling hot so we came back to my house and had a water fight with my Sister.

Had barbecue for din-dins.

Evs read this diary and he said he was impressed.

Anyway, as I sit here, sorry, lie here, scoffing cake, it's 9:52pm and 'Tales Of The Unexpected' is on TV. It's really obvious what is going to happen.

Haven't really had a decent conversation with Louise since Monday. What is this world coming to?

Night night. Mind the bugs don't bite.

Genuinely surprised that I let Evs read this. Diaries were meant to be secret! What was I thinking?

"Mind the bed bugs don't bite" was something my Nan always used to say. I had no idea that bed bugs were real!

Monday, August 20th, 1984

Hello. Did pretty much balls all today. Called for Evs this morning. Didn't do much. Came home and ate dinner. Then went back for Evs. Borrowed his bike, put up the tent and then played swing ball at the Holiday Club on the park.

Went out to a pub with Evs and his Mum in her car. She bought me a lager & lime! I think I'm pissed? Had a toasted sandwich and cake for supper, and now I feel sick. I am lying here in the tent in Evs back garden and we're both writing in our diaries. Mine is much superior of course.

I see Wilko's starring in a film on TV this week called 'The Elephant Man'. I bet Louise enjoys it.

Today I celebrate one week of writing in my diary. Hip hip hooray!

It is now past midnight, so technically it's tomorrow, whoo – crazy man!. I thrashed Evs at 'Yahtzee!' Reading some of his Annuals. I can't really say good night because we're going to stay up until the morning. I will report back on the behaviour of the Dynamic Dickheads (us) tomorrow. What am I talking about? This is tomorrow!

One of the benefits of Evs being so grown up – his Mum happily bought us lager when we were still 13! This was the day we stayed in a tent in his garden, for no real reason other than it seemed like it might be fun to stay awake all night.

Tuesday, August 21st, 1984

Captains Log Star Date 12:04am

Clear air turbulence in hyper-galactic travel. Was space sick in tent (not really). We snuck out of the tent at 3am and walked around the estate. We visited Louise's house but no one was around. So lazy!

Actually I think I have a nagging doubt that she's actually away on holiday somewhere. We went through the school on the way there and it was really dark. We cacked ourselves.

Finally fell asleep for a couple of hours then woke up and had breakfast. Went to the park and went on the rowing boats. We got chased by some townies and so we went and hid on the island. We got badly stung by nettles. Went in the paddling pool and dossed about in the big fountain. Saw my Aunty Jackie and her two youngest kids on the park too.

Staying the night in the tent again tonight, then back to GHQ after that. Just played 'Monopoly' with Evs and his Mum. I came second even though I had Park Lane and Mayfair. We then played 'Yahtzee!' again and this time Evs thrashed us both. I came last.

12:34am now so signing off. Over & out.

I'm not sure that hanging around a girl's house at 3am was an especially good approach to courtship.

Wednesday, August 22nd, 1984

Last night was dead. We were both knackered from the night before and fell asleep about 1:15am.

Had Gooseberry Jam on toast for breakfast, and also Ricicles.

We then tidied up the tent and I went home for my dinner.

This afternoon we went to the Holiday Club again on the park. Benny was there so we dossed about with him. Evs climbed up and sat on top of the phone box. Played Tic for a bit, and then Evs climbed on the roof of the toilets.

He put a milk bottle up there and we threw stones at it. I hit it and knocked it over, but it didn't smash!

Rang Louise again. She wasn't in. She must be on holiday.

There is a program on TV with a black-haired girl called Lucy. She is well fit! She is Scottish and I am a bit in love with her. Don't be jealous Louise. I am forever yours!

Holiday Club was a thing that the local church ran in the school holidays to keep kids occupied while their parents were at work. Free childcare in return for religious indoctrination. Dossing meant to just hang around being bored and getting up to no good.

No idea what the TV show was with the Scottish girl.

Friday November 30th 1984

(The Story Since August 22nd 1984)

Wilko packed Louise in and then Louise went out with Evs (the bastard) for 6 days (Ha! Ha!)

She then packed him in and accused him of using her (not sure what for!)

I've not gone ahead and asked her out for various reasons. The crunch may come soon.

Jayne has developed a sudden liking for me. I quite like her, but not enough. Not as much as I like Louise.

I took Louise's scarf home after Youth Club and put it around my teddy in bed and slept with it on my pillow. God, I love her!

I long for the day when I might get to kiss her.

There will probably be a break from the diary now as we have a long weekend off school and I really need to get a proper book to write in.

I guess I got bored of writing the diary and/or was running out of room in the back of the exercise book. This final entry in this set of torn-out pages comes three months after the previous one and is an attempt to cover all the interesting things that had happened in between times (i.e. not much) before I started the diary proper in its own notebook.

10 December 1984 STATS

Age: 13 years 11 months

Weight: 7 stone 12 pounds

Height: 5 feet 2 inches

Foot: Size 7

Likes: Kiss, Motley Crue, The Young Ones, Louise , Yorkshire Pudding

Dislikes: Wham, Duran Duran, foreign food, smoking, Brookside

Favourite Film: Ghostbusters

Favourite Car: Mini Clubman

Favourite DJ: Mike Read

Favourite Album: Kiss – Double Platinum / Motley Crue – Shout At The Devil

Favourite Single: Motley Crue – Too Young To Fall In Love

Favourite Book: The Secret Diary Of Adrian Mole

The weirdest thing here is that I have no memory of being a fan of the Mini Clubman – but years later when I got my first car – it was a 1975 Mini Clubman. And Brookside was great. What was I on about?

VOLUME ONE

(January 1st 1985 to April 30th 1985)

Tuesday, January 1, 1985

Time: 1:42am

I am pretty knackered. Just watched 'Whistle Test' on TV. I'm in on my own. Everyone else is at a party up the road. I didn't want to go cus it looked boring.

1984 is over. What a year! I went out with Louise and she packed me in for an idiot with a big nose. I've been trying to win her back ever since. I saw her earlier today and she was with her parents on a walk. She went dead red when she saw me and I felt sorry for her. I later saw her friend Jayne and helped her do her paper round. She gave me the impression that Louise didn't like me anymore, so I will try not to follow her around at Youth Club on Wednesday.

It's now nearly 2am and I am freezing cold as the heating went off hours ago. Must go to bed but I'll write again tonight. Good night 1984!

Time: 9:22pm

Minder is on the TV as I write. The main part of today was pretty good. Crawled out of bed just before midday and Ev's came round. He stayed all afternoon and went home about 6pm. Watched Dr. No on TV. Then thought about Louise for a bit. Youth Club on Wednesday could be a crucial turning point.

Back to school on Thursday. What a really heavy bummer that is.

My new year resolutions are as follows and I will come back to cross them out when they are broken during the year

1. ~~Try hard and pass my exams~~
2. Not to worry about any further music exams on my Cornet
3. To stay true to Louise
4. Not to forget about my computer and to keep using it.
5. ~~Not to be taken in by Phillip C's bullshit~~
6. ~~Not to make a fool of myself in front of any girls~~
7. To ignore any feeble advances from Sarah M!
8. To remain friends with Evs and to remember him if I get a girlfriend (i.e. Louise)

That New Year's Eve Whistle Test was great. Strong memories of Big Country playing live from Edinburgh.

Cornet was the instrument I chose to learn at school – because I wanted to stop having piano lessons, and my parents said they would only allow that if I picked up a different instrument. The Cornet seemed small so wouldn't take much carrying – unlike Plonky who chose the Double Bass and pissed his parents right off.

Sarah M was a girl in the year below who fancied me for some strange reason best known to herself.

Also the idea that I "went out with Louise" is, as mentioned earlier, a fanciful embellishment of the truth. It was one dance.

Wednesday, January 2, 1985

Today was quite a let-down really. Evs did not come out during the day and I did sweet F.A at home. I threw my sister out of the shower because I was rushing to get to Youth Club and needed to wash my hair.

I had arranged to meet Evs by the bench but I was late. Evs was even later! We eventually met up and arrived at Youth Club to find the place devoid of life. A notice was on the door that said

"Youth Club reopens Monday 7th January"

We were dead pissed off. Evs bought some chips and we went back to my house. Played 'Jet Set Willy' on the Spectrum and reached tons of unexplored territory. He went home and now I am writing this. I was really disappointed about tonight as I desperately wanted to see Louise. Oh well.

Must stop now – school tomorrow. Boo hiss

Night all.

Ludicrous amounts of pre-mobile phone, pre-internet organisational chaos on display here.

Thursday, January 3, 1985

School today was completely and utterly crap. The only high point was when Stephen H gave me my computer tape with 4 copied games on it. 'Atic Atac', 'Manic Miner', 'Stop The Express' and 'Eric & The Floaters'. The latter will not load so I will have to return it. Jayne and Rachael talk to me but Louise stays away. Pretty sure this means she has definitely gone off me, but I am still madly in love with her. In P.E, Mr Hawkins said *"I'm going to do a foot check"* and I shouted *"mine are still there"*. Mr Hawkins bollocked me.

I helped Jayne do her paper round again and Grandad saw me through the window, and then made jokes about me having a girlfriend. We have got basketball and swimming tomorrow. Boo, hiss. I will try and skive off swimming. I hate it. Everyone who was going on about "who got off with who" at Bridget's party. It was really boring. John A is still off school after having his appendix out. Pygmy has gone back to South Africa. Benny didn't arrive today so the twice weekly rubber wars (where we fire bits of our pencil rubbers at each other in class, using elastic bands) were crap. I got plastered. God knows who Louise wants to go out with. She kept looking over at me during break, but I ignored her. Don't ask me why. Claire B is now officially going out with James and she is going around acting like she is on drugs. I have to go to sleep. Night then.

Foot check was a thing to make sure no one had a verruca. Pygmy was a lad whose Dad kept going out to work in South Africa so he was always in and out of school. He was the shortest kid in the year.

Friday, January 4, 1985

Today I gave Steve H his tape back and he is going to redo it for me. He also says that he will give me a map of "Jet Set Willy and a set of POKEs to go with it. He told me about some new ground called 'The Forgotten Abbey'. It is impossible to get past.

Watched 'Superman II' on the tele although I already saw it at the cinema when it came out.

I went upstairs and when I looked out of my bedroom window there was a layer of snow on the ground. At last it has arrived. I am hoping for much more tonight so that I may be able to miss Brass Band practice tomorrow.

Louise has got chicken pox. I will send her a Get Well Soon card. People are STILL going on about the party. It's all a load of balls if you ask me.

Oh wow! KISS are live on the radio right now! Cool, I am taping it. They are playing 'Strutter'. Ace! To listen to this I must relax and concentrate so I'm going. Bye for now. More tomorrow

---

Games not loading from copied tapes was a common problem. Possibly the worst thing ever – as it took forever to play the tape, and then it would just crash at the end. A POKE was a secret code you could type into the computer to change certain features of the game (usually to give you infinite lives or some other helpful thing).

Saturday, January 5, 1985

Had to get up dead early for Brass Band practice in town. I was totally knackered. Went up to call for Evs afterwards. We came back to my place after he had washed his hair. Played 'Jet Set Willy' but could not get past the stupid Forgotten Abbey. Rang Steve H up and asked him how he did it. He said it took him ages. We then somehow managed to do it straight away! It is dead boring once you finally get to the other side. We went round to Steve H's house at 6:30pm and I got my tape back with 'Cookie' on it. He also gave me a 'Jet Set Willy' Map and a set of POKEs for it. Fred, Harry and Liam called round while we were there. Steve H was dead good and lent me his 'Knight Lore' plus loads of others. Played nearly all of them now and most are shit. Slaphead Sam the Brass Band man told me that I had passed my Cornet exam. What a relief! All that worrying I did.

It is now 12:15am and I am dead bored. I will be playing on my computer all day tomorrow and Evs is not coming out. Get well soon Louise x

---

Brass Band practice was in a disused school gymnasium in town, which had no heating and so was usually freezing cold. Absolute torture at this time of year.

Sunday, January 6, 1985

Jumbo Jobbie Evs came around today after all. Played all of my games now. Tried to copy 'Knight Lore' but it didn't bloody work. School tomorrow. If Louise isn't there I will send her a card. Had a shower this afternoon. Apart from that, today was just crummy. Spitting Image is on tele Yeah! I'm going to bed. Bye for now.

Why is there SO much talk of having showers and washing hair? Why did I think this was worthy of note?

Monday, January 7, 1985

Crappy day today. Chemistry was shit. Annie told me a story about Mr. Flora and that was all that happened. We had a dead boring History homework for tomorrow. I have just finished doing it. We have an Art exam next Monday and a Control Technology exam on Wednesday. I will probably shit them both up. It snowed for the first real time today. It was cool at break times. It is goin to snow again tonight if the forecast is right, but it never is so it will probably all be gone by tomorrow.

Craig B in Art class was hilarious. He is even more on drugs than Claire B when it comes to acting stupid. I helped Jayne with her paper round again and she kept slipping over. Maybe she is also on drugs.

The basketball was just on tele. It was dead exciting. Kingston won after extra-time.

I have to take my Cornet to school tomorrow and I will find out my exam score.

The card is on its way Louise x

I am going now. Bye

I have absolutely no idea what the 'Mr Flora' story was about. I remember a terrible advert for Flora margarine, where a man was desperately mouthing the word "Flora" to his wife through a window as she did the shopping. May have been something to do with that.

Tuesday, January 8, 1985

The card is not on its bloody way. They have only got two 'Get Well' cards and they are both crappy soppy ones.

Took the blower to school and got my exam score. I got 100. A pass is 100. Mum & Dad didn't seem too impressed but sod them

There was no snow last night as I suspected but then there was tons more this morning! None is forecast for tonight, so we will probably get 7 inches by tomorrow.

Scouts was tonight. It was dead crap. I am making a radio. Ha! I was feeling anarchic so I didn't wear my uniform. Because of Scouts it meant that I couldn't go sledging with the lads. Control Technology exam is tomorrow. I will get a dead rubbish mark, I know. It is also Youth Club. Nothing significant will happen there I doubt.

Today during her paper round Jayne told me of her love for Rich H. She must be blind. I have to go now as it's rock hard to write and lie in bed at the same time. Bye!

I don't think 100 was the top score. I wasn't THAT good. I think there was some idiosyncratic scoring mechanism out of 147 or something. Like Snooker.

Wednesday, January 9, 1985

Youth Club was crappy. Louise still has the pox. There was hardly anyone there. Played pool with Evs and of course, I won. Didn't bother watching 'Dallas' in the TV room but instead played netball with some girls instead. Loads of older, bigger youths were waiting to kick us in afterwards, so we climbed out of the gym window and legged it. We got away. There was me, Evs and Richard P. Jayne decided that she wasn't friends with me. Don't ask me why. She is just doing it for attention. Evs did my tape of Knight Lore, Travel With Trashman and Hunchback II. They are skillo!

We had a student Biology Teacher called Mr Beer. He was acting like he was on drugs. Maybe he was drunk. Haha! The Control Technology exam was dead hard. I will not do too badly though. The snow is almost all gone. Hope we have a lot more,

If Jayne wants the cul-de-sac doing by me tomorrow, I will personally shove the newspapers up her alimentary canal (this means arsehole). I am freezing. Goodbye!

Clearly I was paying attention in Biology.

Youth Club ritual was to all cram into the 'TV Room' together and watch the American soap opera 'Dallas' – even though there were a hundred other things to do. I suspect there was no space, and I was just being cool about not getting in.

Thursday, January 10, 1985

Jayne asked me to do the cul-de-sac but the papers wouldn't fit up her arse. I said no anyway, and she did them instead. She then decided that she was friends with me after all and that the reason she wasn't in the first place was because I made some comment when she arrived at Youth Club. God knows what it was. She wouldn't tell me.

We did Rugby in the freezing cold today and I just managed to get away with not doing my Physics homework. RE was crap and Miss Marsh was not here for German so we did balls-all. Tubby got massacred by the supply teacher for messing about.

Jayne still on about fancying Rich H. She is mental.

The snow is all gone. We want an encore! I better go. Bye!

Snow was about the most exciting thing that could ever happen.

Friday, January 11, 1985

Today was dead weird. Silly cows Jayne and Rachael somehow got the idea that I fancied Jayne (untrue!). They then tried to dub me out that she really fancied Rich H and not me. I then said that I didn't give a toss who she fancied. Evs was getting dead pissed off with her, so he did a pretend biting action behind her because of the rumour that she had accidentally bitten someone when they tried to kiss her. We both totally cracked up. Jayne went beetroot and walked off in a huff. We then christened her "Drac". They then planned bitter revenge and said that they all hated me and were sick of me following them around at Youth Club. They also told me that Louise didn't like me. I don't believe this and I never will unless I hear it from Louise herself. Evs got extremely nobbed-off when Drac said that I also followed Evs around all the time. Evs said he would smash her teeth in, but he didn't have a big enough fist! Haha!

Apart from that Miss Marsh was back in but Mrs Trimmer was still off. Swimming was crap as usual and Evs is taping some more games for me. On the way home, we were sitting on the fence when Rich G walked past with his bike. Evs flicked him the Vs, but he saw and came bombing over on his bike and they had a scrap on the grass. Up early in the morning for Brass Band. What a heavy bummer.

"Dubbing someone out" meant to trick them and/or make them look silly. Looking back they were probably right that I did quite fancy Jayne.

Saturday, January 12, 1985

Went to Brass Band and it was shit. Came back. Had dinner.

Evs brought my tapes round and he stayed until tea time.

Watched 'Saturday Live' with Rik & Vyvyan from The Young Ones in it. It was dead funny. All in all today was pretty shit.

Good night!

'Saturday Live' was a British attempt to emulate the long-running US sketch-comedy show 'Saturday Night Live'. This was the pilot episode, so it had received a fair amount of hype in the run-up. Hosted by Lenny Henry, it featured Rik Mayall and Ade Edmonson (aka Vyvyan) doing their 'Dangerous Brothers' routine and the musical guests were Slade and The Style Council.

Sunday, January 13, 1985

Yahoo! Today it snowed again. I hope it will still be there tomorrow for school. Evs came round and we had a right doss pegging snowballs at buses and cars. Art exam tomorrow. I'm drawing the pencil rubber and sharpener.

Played on the computer. Tomorrow the hard revision must start if I am to do well in my exams. I wonder what Drac will be doing (or biting). I better go. Bye!

Monday, January 14, 1985

The snow was ace. School was crap otherwise. Tele was good tonight. Didn't revise after all. Art exam was crap. Totally fucked up my pencil. Balls. Good night!

I assume that this meant I fucked up the drawing of the pencil, rather than fucking up my actual pencil. But you never know.

I used to quite enjoy Art, despite my lack of natural ability. The teacher was really good and kept us engaged for the most part. Although, he did once give me a detention and made me write an essay on the subject of "What is Art?"

After I'd handed it in, he told me the following week that it was so funny he read it to his entire Sixth-Form art class. I wish I could remember what I wrote that was so amusing.

Tuesday, January 15, 1985

Went sledging with Scouts. Cool! Went to the park with the big hill. I almost missed out on going because Slaphead Sam told me I had to go to Brass Band practice. My mum rang him and said we had no car as my Dad was out. Youth Club tomorrow. I predict a boring experience. Find out the truth tomorrow.

I'm pretty sure this was a rare case of my Parents lying for me, and that they just didn't want to have to take the car out in the snow.

Wednesday, January 16, 1985

Time: 5:38pm

About to have my shower for Youth Club. Jayne might talk to me but I doubt it. The thing that annoys me is that just because Jayne isn't talking to me, Rachael isn't either. Louise better do though. She must be back soon. She had chicken pox not the bloody bubonic plague. Us lower formers rebelled against the 6th formers today in the snow. It was cool. Several of them took a good snowball pasting. Youth club now.

Time 10:30pm

My prediction was slightly wrong. Youth Club was totally crap (Louise was absent) but not boring. Jayne managed to speak to me. We played netball and volleyball. But the best news is that Louise is back at school tomorrow apparently!! Whoop! On a more serious note, I got my Control Technology exam result. I got 62%. Not bad for saying I did not do any revision. We had Mr Beer again. He still seemed quite pissed. I had funnels stuck in my ears by him as an "experiment". Got punched by Dave R for shouting *"up yours, ugly"* at him in the corridor when he went past.

Then I went to bed.

Control Technology is probably what we'd call Engineering these days. It was a fun class with loads of practical work – and not a subject I took particularly seriously. Hence I didn't bother revising for the exam.

Thursday, January 17, 1985

Yonder day was reet skill. Lessons were crap but on the way home I was left stranded with Jayne. For a moment I thought she was going to bite me but she had to deliver a paper. I wanted to take our newspaper but she wouldn't give it to me. I pleaded and in the end I told her to sod off, then when I got home I rammed the draught excluder right up into the letter box. She still managed to get the newspaper through though.

The best part of today had to be tonight. I went sledging with Fred, Claire & Annie, and then we also called for Benny. I had my sledge and Benny had his so we had to make do with just two sledges. I am home now and totally knackered. Totally freezing. Going to bed.

PS. Louise is back (and quite blotchy)!!!

Given that I used to have my tea at 5pm and it goes dark about 6pm in January, I assume we must have been sledging in the dark. And that our Parents were fine with this!

Friday, January 18, 1985

Bought Personal Computer Games mag on the way to school. It has a cool map of 'Knight Lore' in it, plus loads of other things.

Matt S has borrowed my copy of 'Knight Lore' and I won't get it back now until Monday.

At dinner break, Rich H was in the wet break room and he asked me to ask Jayne out for him. I did and she said yes of course! She is now dead pleased and talking to me again. I spoke to Louise for the first time since she's been back. Her blotches are almost all gone now.

Benny kept smashing me in, in German and then he got done by Miss Marsh for it.

Brass band tomorrow. Up early. Bum bags!

Knowing Benny he was probably just punching me for being annoying. I was quite annoying.

Saturday, January 19, 1985

Morning: Went to Brass Band. Very boring

Afternoon: Went sledging up the big hill with Fred, Benny, Annie, Kim, James, Sabin, Evs, Claire B, Jackie S, Jayne and Zenia. Dead cool stuff.

Evening: Missed some decent TV programmes and went to see the pantomime. Mum was in it and it was really embarrassing. Me and my Sister were sat in these dead tiny kid seats in the audience. Sarah M kept looking at me, which made me laugh and then she kept going bright red. She is quite fit, maybe I should ask her out but she is dead shy and a year below me. Colin Jones lost the boxing. Pantomime was actually pretty good. I am seeing it again in a fortnight.

My Mum being in the local pantomime was always a source of great embarrassment to me.

Sunday, January 20, 1985

Stayed in bed until lunch time. Ate lunch. Watched tele. Evs called round. We didn't go out. He went home. I had a shower. Ate tea. Watched tele.

I'll have to revise some English now as we have an exam tomorrow.

A pretty archetypal boring Sunday in January. Not even anything on TV good enough for me to mention.

Monday, January 21, 1985

The English exam was pretty easy but we have Maths, Chemistry and History tomorrow. Sarah M was being a pain in the arse today. I nicked off on Rich G's bike while he was having a fight with Evs.

There is a magazine on the top shelf in the Post Office with Samantha Fox in it. She is enormously fit (sorry Louise). Her picture is on the front. There is a small picture of her in my sister's 'Just Seventeen' mag. Oh well on with the revision

---

And herein starts my obsession with Samantha Fox, a glamour model who posed topless in The Sun newspaper in 1983 when she was just 16. The irony being that, in later life, she came out as gay. I never stood a chance...

Tuesday, January 22, 1985

This morning I read the Sun in the Post Office as there is an interview with Samantha Fox and her boyfriend (I hate him!) plus a big photo of her (she has clothes on). Phillip C claims he has a photo of her with her tits out, but I haven't seen it. He says he will bring it to school tomorrow. He probably won't, knowing him. Maths exam was dead easy but tomorrow's will be much harder. Chemistry was rock hard. I will get a dead low mark. History was quite good. I should get a pretty average mark. Didn't take my Cornet to school today because of the exams. Didn't go to Scouts either and didn't want to go to Brass Band because I didn't think anyone would be there on account of the exams, but me and Simon ended up going anyway. It wasn't too bad.

My sister had a fit because she found out I was going on holiday to Paris and Germany etc with the Brass Band in the summer. Dave gave me the real 'Jet Set Willy' map and an 'Atic Atac' map. Pity the computer is knackered. Rich H said today that he didn't like Jayne that much after all and that she is crap at kissing. She didn't bite him though. Second Maths test and Physics tomorrow. More revision.

The computer being knackered is only mentioned in passing but this was a big deal. I had broken it by sticking a fork in the back. Someone told me that was a quicker way of turning it off and on again than going to the plug socket. One blinding flash later and it was totally dead. I never owned up to this.

Wednesday, January 23, 1985

Jockin' Nora! The Maths exam today was rock hard. The thicko classes had an easier paper than yesterday. We couldn't find 1 person in the whole year that thought it was easy. Even Diana and Julia said they thought it was hard. The Physics one was pretty easy apart from the last 2 questions which were on topics we'd not done.

Phillip C forgot the picture. What a surprise. Mr Beer was drunk yet again in Biology.

Tomorrow we have Geography (ok), RE (hahaha). And German (hahahahaha) exams. I'll have to do some Geography revision.

Wanted to go to Youth Club but Mum wouldn't let me. I was supposed to meet Sarah M at the Chippy on the way but I doubt she was there.

Stayed in and thought about Samantha Fox a bit more.

Phil was a well renowned bullshitter who lived up the road from me. It was a real compulsion. He just made stuff up ALL the time. I suspect that every school had at least one Phillip C.

Thursday, January 24, 1985

Geography exam first thing was not too bad but German was the most pathetic thing ever. Claire W didn't answer a single question. I did them all, but I doubt I got any right.

Phillip C forgot the picture yet again. What did I tell you? There was a photo of her in this week's 'Kerrang!' though so I made do with that.

RE exam wasn't too bad but I won't have done very well.

Told Sarah M's friends why I couldn't go to Youth Club last night. The rain has made the new snow go all slushy. It's disgusting. I have revised Biology but we have French first thing tomorrow.

These exams all seem rather pointless, given that I knew I didn't want to take half the subjects at 'O'-Level. My lack of revision effort reflects this.

Friday, January 25, 1985

Quite a good day today. There was supposed to be some aggro between us and the kids from Ralphies at dinner. There were some coppers hanging around at the shops nearest school, so we went up to the big shops instead. It was crawling with pigs when we got there, and a plain clothes told us to go back to school. We ran off up a back jitty but got stopped by a different copper. He balled on about "unlawful assembly" so I just went home. Told Mum I had come straight home. She'd go mad if she knew.

Got German paper result and I got 34 out of 75. This is actually very good! There is still another 25% to come. We didn't have enough time to do the French exam. It's the only one I haven't finished.

Phillip C forgot the picture. AGAIN!

Spoke to Louise twice today. She doesn't have any blotches left now. Did paper round with Jayne again. Count Jayne.

No more revision. Whoop! Brass Band tomorrow (yawn)

I'm loaded with cash now because I got my pocket money. £7.64 to be precise. Good night

---

"Ralphies' was the rival nearby school.

Saturday, January 26, 1985

Went to Brass Band practice in the morning. Went to town in the afternoon and bought 'Two Tribes (Metal Noise Mix)' by Warfare on 12 inch. It's so cool. Much better than the Frankie version.

Going to Nanna's tomorrow and it's my sister's birthday. I have bought her a tool box to use as a make-up box. Well I didn't really as I put no money towards it. Mum paid.

Auntie Jackie, Uncle Brian and my cousins will be there

There is a Beatles film on tele.

I found a copy of The Sun on the bus home and there was another picture of S. Fox in it. Still clothed.

The Beatles film was a dramatisation of The Beatles time in Hamburg called 'The Birth Of The Beatles' not an actual Beatles film.

We had cousins who were the same age as us, and we always looked forward to seeing them (they lived miles away). They were always hilarious and much cooler than we were.

That Warfare cover version of 'Two Tribes' in a punky heavy metal style really was excellent.

Sunday, January 27, 1985

Went to Nanna's house. Quite good. There were 12 of us. It snowed again.

Dad is in a bad mood. Helen fell down the steps at Nanna's house and my Mum pulled the curtains down.

Saw an advert for The Sun on TV and Samantha Fox is in it. She is wearing the same dress as in the photo I saw in the paper yesterday.

Went to bed at 1:25am last night, so going to bed now tired. Sister's birthday was boring.

Not sure how I could proclaim it boring when it was my sister's "legendary birthday where she fell down the steps and then my Mum pulled the curtain rail down by accident".

Only now do I realise that my Dad's bad mood was almost certainly caused by having to spend the day with his in-laws.

Monday, January 28, 1985

We got 4 results today. They are:

Chemistry = 54%

History = 57%

Maths = 44.5%

Art = 63%

I got in trouble for the Maths result.

We will get English, French and Geography results tomorrow. Have to take my Cornet to school tomorrow. Also Brass Band and Scouts. Phil said he brought the picture of Samantha Fox to school today but had put it inside a homework book which he then accidentally handed in. He says he will get it back tomorrow. Rich H said he didn't like Jayne anymore but not to tell her. Me, Evs and Charlie did though. She wasn't too upset thankfully.

Snow from yesterday was gone this morning.

I tended to struggle with Maths, dependent on the teacher at the time. Eventually I ended up getting some private Maths tuition with a lady down the road who was just brilliant at explaining stuff and suddenly it all made sense.

Tuesday, January 29, 1985

Went to Scouts. Firstly went to Brass Band practice. Slaphead Sam doesn't like me and Simon leaving early to go to Scouts.

Got my English result = 79%

I came 3rd highest in the class.

Rich H asked Jayne out again. He is just using her. That's all. Bye.

The Brass Band leader was ex-military and a real stickler. The only way we could fit in Brass Band AND going to Scouts was by leaving Brass Band practice 15 minutes early on a Tuesday. He begrudgingly agreed to this, but EVERY week he made us feel like shit for leaving early.

Wednesday, January 30, 1985

Youth Club today was cool. I'm back in love with Louise. Sarah M can get lost.

Jayne was pissed off with Rich H. He told loads of lies about the stuff they had got up to, and wasn't very nice about her.

Jayne and Louise know that we know something but we can't tell them.

John A asked Ellen out. She's quite fit. She asked me out once when I was totally obsessed with Louise so I said no.

Mr Beer was drunk in class again, and that's about it.

Biology = 79%

French -= 64%

Night.

I'm not sure that Ellen ever did ask me out. More likely she just looked at me once.

Thursday, January 31, 1985

German = 50%

Religious Ed = 57%

Physics = 58%

Not too bad results considering.

Told Louise what Rich H had said about Jayne, and she then told her.

John A is now going out with Ellen (Pengy).

Did paper round with Jayne. She had to go to the dentist.

That's about it. It's Dad's birthday tomorrow and I have got him a bar of chocolate.

Night.

Pengy was our nickname for Ellen because she walked like a penguin, or looked like a penguin. Or possibly both. I'm sure my Dad was thrilled with "some chocolate".

Friday, February 1, 1985

Phil said he was going to buy one of the top shelf mags that has Sam Fox in it.

Then when we got there he didn't have enough money. He said he went back later but they were closed.

Watched two Joan Collins films on TV. 'I Don't Want to Be Born' and 'The Bitch'

The first one was crap, but the second one was better, mainly because you got to see loads of tits.

It was on from Midnight to 1:45am. Now I have to get up for Brass Band at 8:15am

Good night zzzzzzzzzz!

Clearly the nudity in 'The Bitch' was of interest to a 14 year old boy, but I have no memory of the other film – even after looking it up. A 1975 British horror about a demonically-possessed baby. Sounds quite good.

Saturday, February 2, 1985

Can't remember what I did today

A month into Volume One and my commitment to write every day is already waning.

Sunday, February 3, 1985

I can't remember writing last night's entry, let alone what I did.

It was the Pantomime after-party and I got pissed on wine, cider, beer, Vimto, Tizer and cherryade

Sarah M was there. Ho!

Finally told Mum that the computer was broken, so I feel much better now.

That's about it. Good night.

Ah…I think I'm saying that I got pissed the previous night, hence the brevity of the entry. I don't remember the party in question, but I strongly recall the relief I felt at telling my Parents that the computer was broken. I didn't tell them that I did it by shoving cutlery in the back of it. I felt bad when they got all indignant and said they would take it back to the shop for a replacement, because they "paid a lot of money for it!"

Monday, February 4, 1985

My love life is looking up. Not with Louise though. I am not depressed any more.

Everything is TRIFF!

Triff has Ermintrude the tortoise and I have Georgie.

Triff talks to me all the time and Sarah M gets jealous.

Turns out that Phil was telling bulls all along about Sam Fox. He finally showed me a picture today and she was in the bath and you couldn't see anything.

He said if I gave him 40p then he would finally buy the magazine off the top shelf.

That's about all for today. Bye.

Triff was a girl in the year below. One of Sarah M's friends. I gave her the nickname Triff because she used to say 'Terrific!' a lot. I think I just liked her because she had a lot of confidence and was happy to just chat to me about any old rubbish. Nothing ever happened between us, unsurprisingly.

Tuesday, February 5, 1985

Sarah has Ermintrude and Georgie. Triff gave them to her.

Triff cut off Ermintrude's tail.

Phil is still claiming that he will buy the magazine today.

I'm still on top of the world despite having to go to Brass Band and having to take my Cornet to school.

Glee, bliss etc.

I should point out that these are toys animals and not real ones.

Wednesday, February 6, 1985

Everything today was triff.

Including Triff.

Until Dad got home from work and he had a total fit at me for no reason, just like he normally does.

He kept going on about me *wanting* him to hit me, and that being the reason that he wasn't going to?! No idea what he was on about. He's mental.

Youth Club was brilliant! Had a right doss. I've entered a pool competition. Played Netball like a good little girl.

Phil reckons he has given the money for the magazine to Burty's brother. There is an advert in the Trader for a different one too.

The list of people to dream about keeps getting longer.

Sam Foz, Louise, Jayne, Triff, Sarah, Pengy, Jacqui C and Joan Collins. Any more?

Bye.

My infatuation with Triff seems to have lasted 3 days as she is never mentioned again. In retrospect I think my Dad's bad mood was simply caused by me acting like a complete moron, all the time.

Thursday, February 7, 1985

Today was a totally pointless exercise at school. Took my Cornet and my PE kit, and didn't use either of them.

Tonight Annie and Evs called for me and we went up to call for Benny. Then we called for Fred and ended up back at Benny's because he has a spare bedroom they call the games room and we can all hang out there.

Annie had all her photos. They are cool.

Don't know what these photos were, but I guess photos she took at school. Having a camera of your own was quite rare. Benny's games room was amazing and we spent many evenings in there. His Parents were quite well off – evident by the fact that they had an extra bedroom to just give over to him and his mates for general leisure purposes.

Friday, February 8, 1985

Today was the last day in the half term.

It started snowing this morning and but by dinner break it was dead feeble. However it carried on all afternoon and we now have the thickest snow for ages. Going sledging tomorrow.

Phil claims he has now bought the magazine. Mooooooo!

Evs came round tonight and we were so bored we started fighting. He kicked the shit out of me. Tomorrow night his Mum goes to Austria for 2 weeks and he is on his own.

We are going to have a great time round at his house!

Play-fighting was definitely not my idea. Evs was a lot bigger than me (he was a prop forward in the School rugby team!). The fights always ended with my submission. His Mum was a PE teacher at another school, and her Austria trip was with her pupils, I still find it hard to believe that she just left Evs at 14, totally on his own for 2 weeks.

Saturday, February 9, 1985

Snowed dead heavy again last night. It's so deep. Went out with the lads to the sledging hill. Half of them disappeared somewhere else, but the snow was too thick for sledging anyway, so we came home. My Mum had gone to town to fetch the replacement computer. I can't believe they are replacing it when I was the one who broke it (shhh!)

Evs came round for a bit and we played on the new computer. It's the Spectrum + model with hard keys, so even better than the Spectrum I broke.

Evs mum went to Austria at 11pm. It's now 11:40pm.

Evs is on his own!

Finally I admit my guilt over the ZX Spectrum vs Cutlery incident. I was thrilled to bits that they not only replaced it, but they upgraded the model (because they no longer had the old models in stock)

Sunday, February 10, 1985

Woke up this morning and Evs came round. We had some more play scraps (I lost…again) and played on the computer all day.

'The Howling' is on TV on Tuesday and Evs is going to watch it. I bet he craps himself on his own.

'That's Life' is on TV right now. Good night

PS: Added Phoebe Cates to the list.

Not sure why we had such high hopes of 'The Howling' being some amazing and scary horror film. I also don't know what happened to propel Phoebe Cates onto 'the list' of women I found insanely attractive. Maybe I saw Gremlins but didn't think to mention it.

Monday, February 11, 1985

Did pretty much bugger all today.

At the moment I am watching the 'Rock & Pop Awards' on TV. It's cool.

Still in love with Phoebe Cates.

This is what they used to call 'The Brits'. The performers that I thought were "cool" were probably Nik Kershaw and Howard Jones.

Tuesday, February 12, 1985

Went up for Evs and met him and Annie on the way. Benny and the gang came round to go sledging. I was in all my best clothes and got half-killed by Mum when I returned.

Tonight the Scouts had an activity night. There was 9 of us.

Phoebe Cates gets sexier every day.

I am now going to watch 'The Howling' in bed and brick myself to death.

Unclear as to why I was in my "best clothes" on a Tuesday

12 February 1985 STATS

Age: 14 years 2 months

Weight: 8 stone

Height: 5 feet 2½ inches

Foot: Size 7

Likes: Kiss, Motley Crue, The Young Ones, Louise, Samantha Fox, Phoebe Cates, Yorkshire Pudding

Dislikes: Wham, Duran Duran, foreign food, smoking, Brookside

Favourite Film: Ghostbusters

Favourite Car: Mini Cooper

Favourite Album: Motley Crue – Shout At The Devil

Favourite Book: Bachelor Boys – The Young Ones

Weird pivot from the Mini Clubman to the Mini Cooper. I think I might have seen The Italian Job on TV. Almost everyone I know got that 'Young Ones' book for Christmas 1984.

Wednesday, February 13, 1985

Stayed in my pyjamas today until 4pm when Evs came round.

He is pissed off because Annie keeps coming round to his house.

There were only about 10 people at Youth Club tonight. The rest had all gone ice-skating.

'The Howling' was not bad. I didn't exactly shit myself though. Some nudey werewolf ladies in it at one point.

Going to town tomorrow. Might get a new computer game.

Witness how a young boy's disappointment with a horror film is tempered by brief amounts of semi-nudity!

Thursday, February 14, 1985

ST VALENTINE'S DAY

One bloody soppy, measly, crappy Valentine's card today – from Sarah.

The only consolation is that I went into town and bought 'Jasper' for my computer.

It is good but quite hard.

Looked at The Sun in WH Smith. There was also a picture of Sam Fox advertising a heart-shaped see through nightie for Valentine's Day. Unbelievably sexy. I am back in love with her. Sorry Phoebe.

Phil STILL hasn't got the magazine he was on about.

'Jasper' was a very average platform game where you played the main character of a mouse. I was clearly unwilling to admit how bad it was because it was one of the rare times I paid for a legitimate copy of a game. I also needed to make it sound good in order to use it for initiating swaps for other games.

Friday, February 15, 1985

Evs came round in the afternoon. I had a shower and we went into town again.

I bought a Computer magazine. It's pretty good.

Watched a film tonight on TV called 'Berlin Tunnel'. I've seen it before but it's pretty good and dead dramatic.

'American Werewolf In London' is on tomorrow. Amazing!

Good night.

Why do I keep mentioning having a shower??

Saturday, February 16, 1985

Went to town again for the third day running!

Evs bought 'Elite' for his Acorn. It's shit hot!

Stayed at his house playing it until 9pm. Mum was dead worried about me.

Watched 'American Werewolf In London'. It was cool!

Time: Midnight

Good night.

'Elite' was indeed an incredibly addictive space-trading adventure game, albeit painfully slow gameplay. Evs was the only person I knew with an Acorn Electron home computer. We almost all had ZX Spectrums.

Sunday, February 17, 1985

Didn't do much today apart from my homework. Evs didn't come round. Watched 'That's Life' on TV and now I'm going to bed. Shitty old school tomorrow.

'That's Life' was a weird Sunday evening mainstay TV programme. Part current affairs, part consumer safety campaigning, part satirical comedy. Lots of videos of pets doing daft stuff and whole segments on vegetables shaped like genitalia. Almost like a proto-YouTube, but once a week for 45 minutes, and everyone would talk about it at school the next day..

Monday, February 18, 1985

Got up early and had a shower this morning. School was pretty good. I lent 'Jasper' to Steve H.

He didn't like it and gave it to Dave.

Steve J is giving me loads of games and I am lending him some of mine.

Feels like I'm at an emotional high again.

My cover was blown on the 'Jasper' front. Steve H quickly concluded it was shit and didn't hesitate to tell everyone else.

Tuesday, February 19, 1985

School was pathetic today. Got bollocked by Wildey.

Went to Cornet lesson .Went to Brass Band practice. Went to Scouts.

Boring day apart from all the computer games I got off Steve J.

Pancake Day.

The fact I don't mention WHY I got into trouble at school suggests that I probably deserved it.

Pancake Day was another highlight of the year. We were literally overjoyed to be having just some pancakes and lemon juice as our main meal of the day.

Wednesday, February 20, 1985

Today was shit. Got banned from my Computer and TV until Sunday and had to write an essay for Religious Ed.

'Which Way Now?' arrived today.

I love Sam Fox.

The fact I don't mention WHY I got banned from computer/TV ALSO suggests that I probably deserved it.

'Which Way Now' was some kind of educational pamphlet aimed at helping us decide which subjects to take at 'O' Level. It had complex decision trees in it. Stuff like "Do you like trains? Perhaps you should consider being a train driver" or "Are you good at Maths? Perhaps consider going to University and studying Maths".

My year group was the last to do the GCE 'O' Level exams. The following year they changed to GCSEs.

Thursday, February 21, 1985

Today started off crap but then got ace. I overslept and Mum was angry. Forget to take my Cornet to school, so Mum had to bring it to the office. Did 200 sit-ups and killed myself.

Paul S lent me a couple of games but I couldn't use them as I'm still banned. I was dead helpful when I got home and I decided to go and see about getting a paper round.

The real reason for this was because I had seen that Sam Fox was in The Sun again today. I told Phil and he told Paul S, and then Paul S bought a copy. In the photo she is posing with an actual fox. Witty huh? Nanna had given me 50p, so when I went to the paper shop, I also bought a copy. I still asked about the paper round and I now have one starting on Sunday at 7:30am. It will kill me.

I smuggled The Sun into the house down my trousers and Mum & Dad were going to Helen's Parents Evening. On the way out of the door, Dad lifted my ban so I am free again!

I am now more in love with Sam Fox than ever. She is only 4 years older than me, and her nipples are bigger than I expected..

The length of my ban suggests it was serious, and also enough for me to try and impress my Parents by going and asking for a job. But why did I do 200 sit-ups??

Friday, February 22, 1985

Got reports and Option sheets today. I got a good report for some reason.

I decided that I will take French, Biology, Physics, Geography and Control Technology.

Apart from that, school was boring.

I got a book from the library called 'When The Wind Blows'. It's about Nuclear War.. It's a 'Gentleman Jim' type cartoon. It's dead good.

Evs came round tonight and we played on the computer.

Can't stop thinking about Sam Fox

Nothing encapsulates a teenage boy's life in the 1980s more than this entry. Worrying about school, worrying about nuclear war and then thinking about maybe one having sex before the world ends.

Saturday, February 23, 1985

Went to Brass Band practice this morning. Evs came round after dinner and went home before tea.

We had a concert at the Queen's Hall tonight. Identical to the one on December 2nd last year. It was a right doss backstage in the second half when we weren't playing.

Barry McGuigan won the Boxing.

My first ever paper round in the morning.

7am get up.

Having played guitar in bands for years since then, I can totally relate to the bit about having more fun, just hanging out with your mates backstage. The bit where you actually perform is often the least enjoyable part of the evening.

Sunday, February 24, 1985

Did paper round this morning. My round is the three big cul-de-sacs off Evs road. The houses are all massive and they all had the really thick Sunday papers. My bag was dead heavy.

Somehow had 3 magazines left in the bottom of my bag when I'd finished, so I dumped them in a bush.

Did sod all else today.

Good night.

Getting up at 7am on a Sunday killed me every time. I had a Casio MA-5 digital alarm clock that played a rudimentary monophonic 8-bit version of Mozart's Symphony No. 40 In G Minor. I still get a shiver down my spine whenever I hear that piece.

Monday, February 25, 1985

School pretty good. Tomorrow we have from 10:45am to 1:15pm off because of a teacher strike.

Neil from the Young Ones had a new TV program on tonight called 'Roll Over Beethoven'. It's ace.

And so is Sam Fox.

I have no memory of this TV programme. Even after I looked it up and watched clips on YouTube – it doesn't seem familiar in the slightest.

Tuesday, February 26, 1985

Realised that I had a Cornet lesson during the teacher strike but I forgot my Cornet so Rich had to cover up for me. Went to Brass Band and Scouts this evening. Dead boring.

Samantha Fox.

By now I seemed to believe that just by mentioning her name, she might appear in my dreams.

Wednesday, February 27, 1985

Went to Youth Club. It was pretty cool.

The funniest thing was that Louise asked out a kid called Steve. He's a Second Year! Ha ha!

Beat Evs twice at Table Tennis.

School was crap.

Samantha Fox.

Here I am mocking a girl I used to like for asking someone else out, whilst simultaneously dreaming of an impossible relationship with a famous glamour model. Idiot.

Samantha Fox

Thursday, February 28, 1985

School was complete crap.

I finished 'The Sorcerer's Castle' on the computer. Did fuck all else.

I'm now going to Plonky's party. Louise is going to get the piss ripped out of her. Ha!

I sit here listening to Motley Crue's first LP. 'Public Enemy #1'!

Evs got me into Motley Crue, and we went in hard. An obsession with Heavy Metal in general that lasted a good couple of years.

Friday, March 1, 1985

School was shit.

Played on the computer.

Recent times are dead boring with nothing relevant happening at all.

Sometimes Sam Fox is the only thing keeping me sane.

Life really was this dull. The latter comment is probably truer than I realised.

Saturday, March 2, 1985

Brass Band was totally boring.

Went to town in the morning and had a cheeseburger at McDonalds.

Got my paper round again in the morning. What a rip off! Slave labour!

Maybe the News of the World might have a picture of Samantha Fox in it though.

Our local McDonalds had only been open a couple of years, so it was still quite the novelty.

Sunday, March 3, 1985

Dead good.

Got £1.30 in my pay packet for doing my paper round, even though I am only supposed to get 65p. Technically it is only half a round, but as the papers are so fat with magazine supplements on a Sunday they can't fit a full round in the bag. I think they made a mistake. I said nothing.

No Samantha Fox pictures to be seen in any of the papers either.

Evs came round this afternoon. We played on the computer.

Had a shower, did homework and ate a massive dinner.

'That's Life' is on any second.

Good night.

I still feel aggrieved about the paper round issue 40 years later. No way was that half a round. The bag was back-breaking and it took me ages. I quickly realised that the owner's wife would always pay me for a full round, whereas the owner only gave me half. I started to time my return to the shop to coincide with him having his breakfast upstairs, while his kindly wife covered the till.

Monday, March 4, 1985

School was crap as usual.

My History newspaper raised a few laughs. I'm supposed to be going to Plonky's party but I think I might be on Scout camp. Ya! Boo! Sucks!

Watched 'Roll Over Beethoven' again. Dead good.

Yeah, "dead good" – so good I immediately wiped it from my memory.

Tuesday, March 5, 1985

Went to Scouts and Brass Band.

All in all completely boring.

Samantha Fox.

What more can I say?

Wednesday, March 6, 1985

Youth Club. Not bad. Played Netball.

Mr Beer was drunk again and gave us stupid essays to write. He went on about gobbing a lot.

Mr Beer was a training teacher, and we all thought he was great. We obviously equated his "youthful enthusiasm" with "being drunk" because of his name. I hope he never lost that verve. All our regular teachers had clearly been sapped of their lifeforce by us kids.

Thursday, March 7, 1985

Didn't do my Religious Ed homework, as no one else did.

German was a doss. We were chewing up paper and flicking it everywhere using our rulers. All up the walls.

Did my History homework tonight and Evs came round. Played on the computer and I reached a record level on 'Frank N Stein'.

Thought about Sam Fox and went to bed.

Our German teacher as a case in point was quite young, and a bit weird (in retrospect she was just a goth who didn't let being a teacher stop her from dressing like a goth). She had virtually no control of us, and after none of us chose German as an 'O' Level option – her classes became entirely pointless and we repeatedly ran riot like this.

Friday, March 8, 1985

Today was an ace computer freak out. Sinny bought CRASH! With the map of 'Pyjamarama' and most of the playing instructions. The only bit it didn't have was the bit we already knew. Steve J has my copy of the game and Sinny had lent the original to him to copy as it is a hyperload and hard to save from the copy. So Steve lent me the original tape and we will swap on Monday. After a couple of dead close efforts of being killed trying to get the last key, I finally completed it at 90%. It was dead pleasing. Apart from this today was dead boring.

'Pyjamarama' was one of the better platform games, and much to our dismay featured the new hyperload technology which essentially meant making a tape copy was nigh on impossible. The copy always lost just enough quality to stop it loading properly. As you can imagine from all these diary comments on the subject, the games companies were losing huge amounts of money due to the simplicity of copying games.

CRASH! Was a computer magazine dedicated to ZX Spectrum gaming.

Saturday, March 9, 1985

Didn't go to Brass Band practice, as I somehow managed to get out of it.

Did 'Pyjamarama' again when Evs was here.

Paper Round tomorrow. I wonder if I'll get £1.30 again?

I am now going to watch 'Auf Wiedersehn Pet' on TV

Goodbye

PS I love Samanatha Fox

Not that we didn't believe each other, but literally the only way to prove to Evs that I had completed the game was to complete the game AGAIN with him watching.

Sunday, March 10, 1985

Did my Paper Round and got £1.30 in my envelope again. Ha!

In the Mail there was a story about Sam Fox. Luckily this is the paper that my Dad gets, so I didn't have to nick a copy. I will wait until he's read it and nick the page out in a few days before Mum bins it. It has a couple of decent pics.

I'm about to have din-dins. Evs might come round later.

I've done my homework OK, and I doubt I will have anything more to write about tonight.

Good night Sam Fox and thank you the Mail On Sunday

Sadly my parents continued to get the Mail On Sunday for 40 years and ended up as completely radicalised-pensioners.

Monday, March 11, 1985

School was alright. Monday is probably my best school day. I don't have to take my Cornet. No boring lessons. Liam says he will bring 'Automania' for me tomorrow. Tried to copy some other games, but it never seems to work here. Evs will have to do it for me. He has a better tape recorder.

Tomorrow will be a crap day I know.

We didn't have a music centre with integrated tape-to-tape decks, so my attempts to copy games involved connecting my crap tape recorder via a dodgy cable out of the headphone socket – into the microphone socket of my sister's even crapper tape recorder. No wonder it rarely worked.

Tuesday, March 12, 1985

Had my Cornet lesson at school. Then went to Brass Band practice after school, but not Scouts.

Apart from that today wasn't as bad as I feared.

The girls were all taken out of class and given a talk about the birds and the bees. Afterwards they said they had been shown loads of pictures of boys with big dicks.

I remember that some of the girls found it hilarious while some seemed truly distressed by it all.

Wednesday, March 13, 1985

School was quite good. Out last ever lesson with Mr Beer was marred by a test.

I didn't go to Youth Club but instead went to the cinema to see 'Purple Rain' with my sister.

There were quite a few of us there. James was snogging Katie, Matt was snogging Debbie and John was snogging Pengy.

I just watched the film.

It was shit hot. Prince is ace. The songs were cool and the film was dead emotional.

Got a lift back with Rich's Dad.

I'm sure that "just watching the film" was what Prince would have wanted.

Thursday, March 14, 1985

Evs brought his tape recorder round tonight and I have saved some games. I still have some more to do though.

School was pretty boring. Skived off French by going to Brass Band practice and Miss Farnsworth was absent for Religious Ed.

Dossed about in German as usual.

Concentrated in Physics.

Had my interview with Mr Lawrence. I am down for 'O'-Level in everything on my Options sheet.

Sam Fox is lovely.

Is she? I should have mentioned it more often.

Friday, March 15, 1985

Had Cross-Country today and it killed me off. I hate running long distance.

German was crap, so was Maths, did sweet FA in Library and we watched a film in Music.

Copied a few more games but couldn't get 'Underwurlde' to work.

Aunty Iris is coming tomorrow to buy us our Easter presents.

I might ask for 'School Daze'. It looks good.

We had a childless Aunt who insisted on buying us "Easter Presents" as well as gifts at Christmas. We thought this was normal at the time. It was always hotly anticipated as we could essentially ask for stuff that we knew we'd never get our Parents to buy us....

Saturday, March 16, 1985

Aunty Iris came. I got a top from Burtons and some cool trousers from C&A.

Helen got a ton of clothes from Miss Selfridge. Miles more stuff than me, so I got 'Everyone's A Wally'

It is an ace game. Coolness.

We won a match for once, and now I'm watching the Boxing. Good night.

Thanks a million Aunty Iris!

...like "cool trousers" obviously.

'Everyone's A Wally' was the sequel to 'Pyjamarama' and had only just been released. I was the first kid in our class to get a copy

Sunday, March 17, 1985

Got up and did my Paper Round. Dead boring.

Went to church for the Scouts Parade. Dead boring.

Played on 'Everyone's A Wally' and earned £50.

Watched 'That's Life' and 'Spitting Image' on TV

Evs couldn't come out so I did fuck all else.

I should clarify that I earned £50 in the game and not in real life.

Monday, March 18, 1985

School was totally crummy. The only good thing is that 'The Young Ones' is back on TV in a minute.

I have the tape recorder ready next to the TV speaker. They are showing all 12 episodes starting at the beginning this week.

Shit hot!

Dave is bringing 'Tir Na Nog' round tomorrow.

To explain – we did not have a Video Recorder at this point (in fact we didn't get one until the week before the 'Live Aid' concert in July 1985) so we couldn't record our favourite programmes to watch again. All we could do was record the audio by sticking the cassette player next to the TV. There was an art in positioning the cassette player with its in-built microphone close enough to the TV's speaker so that it picked up the sound without being too quiet or so loud that it distorted.

Tuesday, March 19, 1985

Dave brought the original tape of 'Tir Na Nog' round today. It's shit hot! The best game I have played in ages. It would be crap without the well-drawn map in CRASH! Mag though. I haven't copied it yet.

School was crap. So was Brass Band. Didn't go to Scouts as they were having a boring film show from Pete.

I'm now going to listen to my tape of last night's episode of 'The Young Ones'!

Not sure why I was so into 'Tir Na Nog' as I seem to remember it was quite boring, and consisted of a caveman lolloping around aimlessly.

Wednesday, March 20, 1985

Steve lent me 'Airwolf', 'Zip Zap', 'Sabre Wulf', 'Finders Keepers', 'Beaky & The Egg Snatchers', and 'Blue Thunder.'

'Airwolf', 'Beaky', 'Sabre Wulf' and 'Finders Keepers' are worth copying.

The school Brass Band concert went quite well.

Skived off Control Tech to attend the practice before.

The rest of the school day was boring.

Inter-house Cross Country race tomorrow. Bad karma man.

Although I detested long-distance running, the school Cross-Country route took us all over the estate, through fields and down various footpaths. It also gave most of us a chance to stop running as soon as the school was out of sight, and enjoy a pleasant walk in the countryside..

Thursday, March 21, 1985

Inter-house Cross Country was bum. Came 56th in our year. I hate running.

Copied 'Tir Na Nog'

Watched 'Top Of The Pops'. Billy Bragg was on and he was ace!

'Only Fools and Horses' is on now. Also ace at the moment.

New Motley Crue album is out soon and I'm getting it. Good night.

Here we see the start of the musical schism that took place between the old me ("heavy metal forever") and the new me ("ooh I can actually relate to this alternative/indie music a bit more than stuff about shouting at devils"). Billy Bragg really did change my life playing 'Between The Wars' on Top Of The Pops that night.

Friday, March 22, 1985

Accidentally slashed my finger open on a razor blade in German today so it's hard to write.

Sam Fox and Lee Aaron our now in a battle for my favourite. Sam Fox probably wins, although the pictures of Lee Aaron in Kerrang are great!

Evs came round tonight and we had another wicked fight. I'm knackered. He won.

School was crap. Good night. My finger really hurts.

Why did I have a razor blade in a German lesson?

I don't think I had actually heard any of Lee Aaron's music. I didn't need to.

Saturday, March 23, 1985

Brass Band this morning was bum.

The dance tonight was pretty good. My sister got off with Johnny M. Ha!

Went to McDonalds with the gang. I chewed up my second McDonalds straw of the day as I also chewed one up in McDonalds in town with Evs earlier.

Bought the Billy Bragg single £1.25 and also bought a computer mag.

Now in bed. Paper Round in the morning.

Oh no!

If you aren't in any doubt yet as to the boredom at play. Chewing up straws in McDonalds had entertainment value, and will be mentioned several more times.

Billy Bragg always had "Pay no more than.." pricing on his sleeve art, so that record shops didn't rip you off by adding a ridiculous margin. £1.25 was very cheap for a 4-track 7" single.

Sunday, March 24, 1985

Didn't do my History homework. I'll forget my book tomorrow.

Paper Round killed me.

Found loads of new ground in 'Finders Keepers'.

Pam & Ken came this morning. Dead boring.

Chicken for dinner.

'That's Life' is on TV now.

Good night.

Pam and Ken were some of my Mum's ancient cousins. We had chicken for dinner? Thank god I recorded THAT fact.

Monday, March 25, 1985

"Forgot" my History book.

Dead uneventful.

2 tapes of games off Steve, 1 tape off Dave and 1 off Paul S. Cool.

Haven't played them all yet though.

Went out with the lads tonight. Right doss.

Just taped 'The Young Ones'. Now I'm going to listen to it again in bed.

It wasn't unusual to record the audio of 'The Young Ones' and then immediately listen back to it. The tapes got played to death and me and my sister would memorise every word. It still feels odd to watch the episodes now and find I know the words, but have totally forgotten the visuals that they accompanied.

Tuesday, March 26, 1985

School totally and utterly bum bag.

Cornet lesson boring.

Brass Band practice boring.

Didn't go to Scouts.

Saw Johnny M at Brass Band but my sister didn't believe me.

Played on computer.

Now I'm going to listen to 'The Young Ones' in bed.

This entry was accompanied by a rudimentary sketch of the characters.

Wednesday, March 27, 1985

School was totally crap.

Youth Club was a pretty bum vibe too.

Got a wicked chest infection, so I think I will try and skive school tomorrow.

My reference to skiving suggests that I wasn't quite as ill as I made out.

Thursday, March 28, 1985

I really am actually ill now. Off school.

Been to the Doctors and I'm now not going on the Scout camp.

At least I won't miss the next episode of 'The Young Ones'.

More tomorrow.

Signed:

The Ill Ones

OK maybe I must have been pretty ill for my Mum to have sent me to see a Doctor. Unless she was just calling my bluff. Will I survive?

At least I was well enough to draw a little pentagram at the end of this entry.

Friday, March 29, 1985

I am more ill than ever before. Sore throat et al.

Went to the Post Office at lunch time and saw the guys. They all called me a skiving bottom boil.

Evs came round tonight and we did loads of ace things on 'Everyone's A Wally'. Earned £520!

Rest of today, dead boring.

Cough.

So, so ill. So very ill that I'm up and walking to the shops and then having a friend round to play computer games all evening…

Saturday, March 30, 1985

Boy am I ill. Cough, bloody cough. Did jack all today but Evs came round tonight and he took 'Dark Star' and 'Beaky & The Egg Snatchers' back to Steve's house.

Evs told him I was ill and dead bored, so Steve has lent me a great case full of 77 games!

It's going to take me years to get through them all.

Good night.

Unbelievable scenes to be suddenly presented with so many games to play. I remember it was a big cassette storage case full of games that I'd never even heard of.

Sunday, March 31, 1985

A lot of Steve's games are crap but some are all right.

Went to Nanna's after dinner. My cousins have been there since Friday night. Dead good!

Sis did my Paper Round this morning. She had to get up at 6am really because the clocks have gone forwards. Ha!

April Fool's Day tomorrow. I've got to think of loads of dead ace tricks to play.

Good night.

And still so ill that my poor Sister had to do my paper round for me.

Monday, April 1, 1985

Totally shit day. Did no April Fool's tricks at all.

Made a shitty recording of tonight's episode 'Bomb'. Typical. The best ever episode of 'The Young Ones' and I mess it up.

To cap it all off, I've got a really runny nose.

Sniff.

And here we have an example of the TV audio recording method going horribly wrong. You had no idea that you'd messed up until you'd pressed stop, rewound the tape and then listened back. I took this particular incident very badly.

Tuesday, April 2, 1985

Still depressed about my recording of 'The Young Ones'. Never mind.

My nose is much better today.

Went to the shopping centre. No good books in the library. Went in the Newsagent to look for CRASH! Magazine. They didn't have it.

Cleo Rocos off the Kenny Everett show was on the front of The Sun, she was having her dress ripped off by an old fogey. It said "more on Page 2", so I turned the cover to look and there on Page 3 was Sam Fox! Surprise! I bought a copy and snuck it back into the house.

I am looking at it now.

Yes. "Looking at it".

Wednesday, April 3, 1985

Mum wouldn't let me go to Youth Club Roller-skating party.

Did jack all in the day.

Went to bed.

Completely boring.

Got some new trainers and football boots. That's all.

Oh, and I bought CRASH!

I have always been crap at skating, and I've always hated it, so I don't know why I seemed so aggrieved at not being allowed to go roller-skating.

Thursday, April 4, 1985

Dead good. Went round to Evs. We went into town and chewed up a straw in McDonalds.

Tonight was Plonky's party. Willis managed to break two chairs and got really pissed. Then we all got chucked out. My sister got off with Andy. Her friend Cheryl got off with Liam.

We went home and James & Andy had to ring up their Dad from the pay phone to say it had finished early and could he pick them up.

Went home and the phone rang. I answered and a woman said "Is Kevin there?" I said "no" and she hung up. Then she rang back again and I picked up but didn't say anything.

She kept saying "Hello?, Hello?"

And eventually I just said "Look, Kevin is NOT here" and hung up.

Good night.

Cheers!

Quite a legendary party. Plonky's parents were away for the night so it was always going to end in carnage. My sister was two years above me at school so to see her and her friend kissing boys in my class was pretty horrifying.

Friday, April 5, 1985

Did pretty much balls all today.

Went round to Evs this morning.

He is getting totally boring. Just plays 'Elite' all day.

Cleaned my bike in the afternoon. Dad made me.

Watched TV and then went to bed.

I love Samantha Fox.

As mentioned, 'Elite' was quite an addictive game but single player and very slow, therefore a miserable spectator sport.

Saturday, April 6, 1985

Stayed in bed this morning to watch 'Saturday Superstore'.

Played on the computer all afternoon.

Watched 'Blazing Saddles' on TV. It's a dead funny film.

Later I watched 'Little Big Man' about Custard and Hat Stands. This finished at 12:45am.

I supposed to have my paper round in the morning and I am not setting my alarm.

A weak joke about Custer's Last Stand, but 'Little Big Man' is a great film.

Sunday, April 7, 1985

Mum had a fit this morning because my alarm didn't go off.

I still had to go in and do my Paper Round though. Pete gave me a measly 65p in my envelope.

I read in the News Of The World that Sam Fox has packed in her boyfriend. She must have heard about me. Ha!

There was a small picture of her, but I thought I better not steal the paper. At least it gave me something to look at and something to enjoy in my work!

I've just had a shower even though I didn't want one. Dad had a massive fit to make me.

I think we are going to see boring Aunty Iris today.

God help me!

Must have timed my return to the paper shop wrong on top of everything else. I guess if my Dad was forcing me to have a shower I must have stank. I also note that my Aunty is now "boring" when there are no 'Easter Presents' involved.

Monday, April 8, 1985

Dead good day! Watched 'The Muppet Movie' on TV this morning and various other things.

Evs and Cheryl came round this afternoon. Had a right doss when Mum & Dad went out, we stole all my sisters toys and then had a big fight with them both trying to get them back. I think Evs fancies Cheryl. Her tits are massive. Easily the biggest in my sister's year.

Watched 'The Revenge of The Pink Panther' and 'The Cannonball Run' earlier. They are both ace films. Yawn. Tired now.

Good night.

This was Easter Monday and back then, they would make an effort to put good films on all day.

Tuesday, April 9, 1985

Went for a bike ride this afternoon. Called in the Newsagents and there was another mag on the top shelf with Sam Fox in it.

Phil rang for me while I was out. I wonder if it's about the Sam Fox mag? He was totally bullshitting about the previous one. He must have been. He never had it.

Dad is totally narked off with me and I have to go to bed early tonight. 9pm.

Boo hiss.

It's just all boredom and tits isn't it?

Wednesday, April 10, 1985

Dragged myself out of bed and went up to call for Evs at his house. We then went into town. We chewed up more McDonalds straws. I bought a quarter of toffee.

Came home and did sweet FA.

Had a shower and went to Youth Club. Yet again we forgot that it wasn't on in the school holidays.

Me, Claire, Kim, Fred, Dave and Plonky went to Hannah's house because Plonky fancies her.

Dave & Kim, and Claire & Fred were snogging, so me, Plonky, Hannah and Mandy fucked about (not literally) in the other room.

Bed now.

This is the first mention of Hannah. She would go on to play quite an important part in my life. Me and Plonky BOTH fancied her, I'm just not admitting it here.

Thursday, April 11, 1985

Watched 'The Omen III' last night when I got home.

Had a lie-in this morning.

Didn't go out all day because it was raining. Nanna & Grandad came to visit and that really pissed me off.

Played 'Fred' and 'Mr Wimpy' all afternoon with pokes.

Went to bed.

Again, I feel bad for not appreciating my Grandparents' visit. Both of the games I mention were pretty crap, so I must have been desperate to avoid dreaded human interaction.

Friday, April 12, 1985

Did fuck all.

Moped around and played on the computer all day.

Did bugger all.

This Easter holiday was quite the riot eh?

Saturday, April 13, 1985

Watched TV in bed all morning.

Beryl from across the way gave me & my Mum a lift into town.

She failed her driving test yesterday and I can see why. She is crap at driving.

Bought a computer game for £1.99 called 'Murder At The Manor'. It's a mediocre adventure game.

Had a phone call from the Scout leader tonight. There is a Camping practice tomorrow morning at 9:15am.

Ugh!

'Murder At The Manor' was really bad, and judging by the price, this must have been in the sale because no one wanted it.

Sunday, April 14, 1985

Got up dead well and did my Paper Round. Came back and got ready and went to the meeting place in the car park for 9:15am. It was devoid of life.

9:20am went home.

9:21am saw Simon on the way home and he said it was all still on.

9:25am back in the car park.

Everyone turned up at 9:30am. I had just remembered the time wrong.

Me, Simon, Rob C, Horrors, Ian and Sarah C. Went up into the hills and the countryside. Sarah C's driving is totally reckless! Crapped myself.

Walked on some moors, saw some sort of stone circle. Came back. 10 miles hiked in all. I'm knackered. School tomorrow.

Oh! Boo!

For saying life was otherwise so clearly boring, it seems strange that I have no memory of this Scouting adventure.

Monday, April 15, 1985

First day back at school was complete cattle business. Load of codswallop.

Came home. Missed 'Roll Over Beethoven' but did manage to tape 'The Young Ones'. It was blummin' brilliant. The episode was called 'Boring'.

The recording turned out dead ace, so that was a relief after last time.

FTUMSH!

Good night!

"FTUMSH" is simply a reference to an incidental character in this episode of 'The Young Ones'

Tuesday, April 16, 1985

No Cornet lesson or Brass Band practice today because Samuel is in South Africa teaching all the little black kids how to toot on their horns.

Scouts was blummin' brilliant! We are going on a camp. Me, Colin, Gav, Simon, Rob and Piggy.

School was wanky doodle dandy.

Good night my little ones.

I think I imagined him as a humanitarian in the townships, but in reality this was during Apartheid so it's entirely possible that I may have got that one horribly wrong.

Wednesday, April 17, 1985

School was alright apart from French. Didn't go to Youth Club but stayed at home instead.

Had a shower and did fuck all else.

Good night Sam. Hello Samantha!

This business with continually documenting my showers is just confounding me now.

Thursday, April 18, 1985

School was really boring!

Played guitar on the field with Ian and Anthony.

Kerrang came and on the centre pages was…not Lee Aaron, not Sam Fox but….FIONA!

Who?

She is a fit new woman singer who I have never heard of or seen before, but she is very fit.

Maybe even more than Samantha Fox.

As with Lee Aaron, I don't think I ever heard any of Fiona's music. At this point, I couldn't really play the guitar, although we had been given a battered acoustic by a neighbour. I was desperately trying to learn and I would watch these two lads like a hawk because they were pretty accomplished. I'd go back home and try to copy what they played.

Friday, April 19, 1985

Did fuck all at school.

Went to Colin's house for a meeting about the forthcoming camp.

Watched 'Rollerball' and 'The Howling' at his because he has a video player.

Came home.

Went to bed.

I remember seething with jealousy at any of my friends who had video recorders. I must have badgered my parents quite hard, as we ended up getting one 3 months after this.

Saturday, April 20, 1985

Got up and went to Brass Band practice in the morning.

Went into town this afternoon. Got a blank tape for copying games and went to the bookshop.

Looked through a few medical books.

Came home, ate dinner, watched TV, wrote this and went to bed.

"Looking through a few medical books" was really a covert way of saying that I was desperately trying to find anatomical displays of the human female form. We needed diagrams dammit!

Sunday, April 21, 1985

Did Paper Round and then came home and did my homework.

Apart from that, did fuck all else.

Watched 'Goldfinger' on TV.

Went to bed.

Happy Sunday!

Monday, April 22, 1985

Got given a 50 word essay to write on the subject of "silence" in Maths.

School was shit.

Now watching 'The Young Ones' and it's brill.

Good night.

As far as I remember the subject of the punishment essay was chosen because I wouldn't shut up talking.

Tuesday, April 23, 1985

I have to save space now until pay-day so I can afford to buy a new notebook for the next volume of my diary.

Went to Brass Band.

Did a ton of homework, including an essay for History.

Camping on Saturday and then Alton Towers on Sunday.

At least that means I ain't doing my Paper Round or going to Brass Band practice, or going on the St George's Day Scout Parade.

Got given a Form Point today!!

Now going to listen to my recording of last night's episode of 'The Young Ones'. It's called "Interesting". Totally potty!

Good night.

The visit to Alton Towers was with the Brass Band. We would play in the bandstand all morning (to absolutely no one) and then get the afternoon free to go on all the rides. A "form point" was I think a good thing. I never mention getting another one.

Wednesday, April 24, 1985

Youth Club was crap.

Did fuck all at school and decided to save space here…

Good night.

The reference to saving space was because I was nearing the final few pages of this notebook. Clearly I was anticipating more exciting days to come.

Thursday, April 25, 1985

School was crazy. In German, the teacher went out and left us to do work. Claire W dared me to put my hand up her skirt. She said she bet I wouldn't dare touch her knickers, and then when everyone egged me on, and I finally did it – she screamed! I was really embarrassed and tried to look innocent.

Went to town after school and bought CRASH!

---

*This is a very bizarre memory. I strongly recall **not** wanting to do this (because it seemed completely wrong) whilst at the same time being totally intimidated by her firm coercion (and everyone else surrounding me making chicken noises). I guess she picked on me as the person most likely to start crying rather than take the dare. I was quite scared of Claire W anyway and this incident made that even worse.*

Friday, April 26, 1985

Had a right doss in German messing about with balloons. Claire W had a pair of jeans on today, thank god.

Tomorrow I venture into the wilderness on our camping expedition.

If I do not return, please let Sam Fox, Lee Aaron, Fiona and Louise that I love them.

This is the first time in two months that I've mentioned Louise so I guess I'd largely moved on from that particular infatuation.

Saturday, April 27, 1985

Camping. God I am knackered out!

Sunday, April 28, 1985

God I am cold and knackered. What a weekend!

Kind of annoyed that I didn't detail anything that happened, as I can't remember this Scout camp at all. I can't even remember where we went, but I guess it involved a lot of hiking and a lot of carrying camping equipment on our backs.

Monday, April 29, 1985

Can I last 'til the end of the month? I haven't got a new diary yet.

'The Young Ones' was ace. It was "Flood".

Tuesday, April 30, 1985

Today is the last day of the month so I will get a new diary tomorrow, meaning I can start it on May 1st.

Got given 2 sides of A4 lines by Mrs Kirk (bitch).

Brass Band was a no-go but I went to Scouts.

Got 20/20 for my Radio test. I'm now officially an APL

Got my radio working and everything is brill.

APL = Assistant Patrol Leader I think? Anyway – here we are at the end of Volume One, having written every day for 120 days, in varying levels of detail, about fairly consistent levels of boredom.

VOLUME TWO

(May 1st 1985 to March 1st 1988)

Wednesday, May 1, 1985

Welcome to the Pleasure Diary Volume II! By Mark goes to WH Smith to buy a new Silvine notebook.

Handed in my French lines today and the stupid cow didn't even look at them, just ripped them up in front of me and threw them in the bin.

School was otherwise uneventful and so was Youth Club. Played 5-a-side football and then we all went up to Hannah's house. Campaigned for M.O.P and then listened to an LP of dirty Rugby songs that her Dad had. Something about fists, kite strings and ducks. Pure filth.

Got some chips, came home and went to bed.

I do enjoy my indignation at the teacher not even looking at the work I did as a punishment. Did I really think she cared?

No idea what M.O.P is or was.

Thursday, May 2, 1985

Got up, had breakfast, cleaned my teeth, went to School. Did bugger all. Had dinner. Did bugger all, came home, had tea, watched TV, cleaned teeth, went to bed.

A day in the life of Mark. By Mark.

But I can't help notice that I didn't have a shower. Hmmm. Interesting.

Friday, May 3, 1985

School was pretty good. Mr Hawkins was away for Maths, and we did our "We Are The World" in Music, featuring me being brilliant on the piano.

Anthony lent me "The White Album" and "Abbey Road" by The Beatles.

Did fuck all in PE and German.

Went out tonight with Benny, Fred, Plonky, Harry and Gav. Played football on the park.

Claire and Hannah came down and we all dossed about. Got in at 10pm.

Watched TV for a bit and went to bed.

My proficiency on the Piano is a long way from "brilliant", so I guess that was sarcasm. Being lent those two albums was a pretty formative moment. Anthony went on to show me how to play half the songs on guitar (the easy half obviously).

Saturday, May 4, 1985

Got up for Brass Band practice this morning. Saw Fred on the bus.

Got to the place only to find that there was no one there. Came home, very pissed off.

Might go back into town this afternoon, but I doubt it.

Eurovision song contest tonight. Our song is crap and sung by a middle-aged woman called Vikki.

I am going into town after all.

Paper Round tomorrow. Ya! Boo! Sucks!

This was a pretty forgettable UK Eurovision entry (even though it came fourth). Unless Vikki has fiddled her Wikipedia entry, she was only 26, so my "middle-aged woman" slur seems harsh. However, I just watched the video on YouTube and I stand by every word. They dressed her like an Aunty at a wedding.

Sunday, May 5, 1985

Got up and did Paper Round.

Came back home and felt really ill. I spent the rest of the day in bed. I feel a bit better tonight, but still not 100% yet.

Here is a list of all the fit women I have seen on TV or in Kerrang lately.

Sue Robbie
Sam Fox
Lee Aaron
Linda Lusardi
Fiona Flanagan
Sharron Davies
Susan Dando
Katie Mac
Hollie Laird
Nicole Peeples
Apollonia
Phoebe Cates

Quite a long list there, but so what. They are all fit. Good night.

I had to google some of these. A strange list, and I think proof that, as a hormonal teenage boy, I could probably have been turned-on by a packet of Corn Flakes.

Monday, May 6, 1985

Bank Holiday today.

Went to call for Evs this morning and his Mum took us up to the Water Club and we played Pool all afternoon.

Evs came up to mine tonight and we dossed about.

Now I feel ill again.

I think the "Water Club" was a place with a big lake where she did sailing. Not sure where it was, or why we only played Pool and didn't go in the water.

Tuesday, May 7, 1985

I feel better. Went to school and had my Cornet lesson. Slaphead Sam wants me to have private lessons at his house.

Went to Brass Band and Scouts. Got told off at the latter for being bored.

I'm a bit knacked out so I'm off to bed now.

Adults were always telling us off for being bored. We couldn't help it!

I did end up having private lessons too, and eventually passed Grade 5 theory and practical exams. I can't remember exactly when I stopped playing, but I think it was when I left school in July 1987.

Wednesday, May 8, 1985

Decided not to go to Youth Club today because it's dead boring these days.

Dave lent me a computer tape with 'The Hobbit' and loads of other games on it. Mostly dead boring ones.

Another truism – a lot of Spectrum games were terrible and you often played them for less time than the tape took to load.

Thursday, May 9, 1985

Miles got knocked down by a car today outside the shops.

Apart from that today was v. boring.

Good night.

I can't actually remember anyone called Miles, so I hope they were OK. I don't mention it again.

Friday, May 10, 1985

Dossed about loads in German today.

I'm going up to call for Benny now so I have to go. More tomorrow.

Our poor German teacher…

Saturday, May 11, 1985

Brass Band practice this morning was utter bum!

Went to Evs this afternoon but he got bollocked by his Mum and I got chucked out.

Came home. Watched a bit of '10' with Bo Derek. She wasn't in the bit I saw, but pretty much everyone had their tits out. Also the odd fanny.

Paper Round tomorrow. Boring.

Strangely I never considered a career as a film reviewer.

Sunday, May 12, 1985

Just done my Paper Round. 65p. Boring

Nicked a copy of one of the Sunday supplements as it has some pictures in it of Princess Stephanie of Monaco in a swim suit.

Homework this afternoon, Boring.

I had forgotten all about Princess Stephanie. She was a regular in all the newspaper gossip columns in the Eighties. The glamorous daughter of Grace Kelly and Prince Rainier III, but you rarely see her name these days. I just had to check she wasn't dead. She's alive. Relax.

Monday, May 13, 1985

School was really just an utter bummer.

Watched 'The Young Ones' tonight. It was the brilliant episode 'Bambi'.

Copying loads of games with Evs tape recorder at the moment. Moon Cresta, Baseball etc

---

I guess that Evs didn't need his tape recorder all that much, as the only Acorn Electron owner in our class, there was no one for him to swap games with. I really took advantage of his kindness and copied as many games as I physically could.

Tuesday, May 14, 1985

Went to Brass Band Practice but not Scouts as Simon has got tonsilitis. We have a big concert on Saturday night.

School was really boring. Nothing interesting happened at all today.

Another lovely pictorial annotation for this entry.

Wednesday, May 15, 1985

Didn't go to Youth Club.

Copied 'Chuckie Egg II'. It's pretty good.

Everton won the European Cup Winners Cup. It was an ace match and the score was 3-1. Rapid Vienna are a crap team.

I haven't had a shower like I'm meant to, but they can't tell me off as I'm asleep in bed now!

Ha! I've upped the ante now and I'm logging showers I DIDN'T have.

Thursday, May 16, 1985

Had the shower I was meant to have yesterday.

Apart from that, nothing to report. Boring.

Phew! The shower went ahead as planned. I sense that your relief is palpable, dear reader.

Friday, May 17, 1985

Me and Evs went up to Benny's house, then we went out. Dossed about on the park and got chased by Mr. Anaemic.

At school today Tubby threw my bag out of the top floor window and it almost hit the caretaker. He gave it to the Deputy Head and I had to go and fetch it and explain what happened. Tubby has to own up to doing it on Monday or we will both be dead men.

Good night.

The name "Mr Anaemic" sounds familiar but I can't picture him. Did every school have an 'angry bloke on the park who used to harass the kids'?

Saturday, May 18, 1985

Went to Brass Band this morning and had our photos taken.

Watched the FA Cup final. Man Utd won and Everton lost. Ha!

Did our concert at the Salvation Army hall. It was pretty boring. About 70 people in the audience, including the little baby that cried throughout.

Went to bed.

Not sure why I expressed glee at Manchester United's victory at the expense of Everton. I have no allegiance to either team, and earlier in the week I had been rooting for Everton in the European game.

Sunday, May 19, 1985

Just about managed to get up for my Paper Round. I got given £1.30 for the first time in ages.

Went to see my boring Godmother and her two pain in the arse kids. It was totally boring but she gave me a bar of chocolate, so it wasn't too bad.

'That's Life' is on TV now so I'm going to bed.

Still to this day I will forgive anyone anything for a bar of chocolate.

Monday, May 20, 1985

School was v. boring. We had a good doss about in Art and Drama but had to do proper work the rest of the day.

Me and Steve are starting a computer games company called 'Mega-Looney Software' and we are halfway through our first ever game. It's called 'Cornelius The Worm'. It's ace.

Watched 'The Young Ones' tonight and it was 'Cash'. Brilliant!

Night night.

It was a bold venture, considering that neither of us had any skills beyond very simple BASIC programming, nor did we have any idea who to produce, market or distribute a computer game. The game involved a worm, which I think Steve managed to crudely animate going across the screen.

Tuesday, May 21, 1985

School was complete crap. Mega Looney Software had a board meeting at my house at lunchtime. Me, Steve and Dave.

Went to my Cornet lesson, Brass Band and Scouts.

They were all mostly boring.

No more to say tonight. Good night.

A board meeting no less! Not sure what Dave brought to the table as he had even less computer skills than us.

Wednesday, May 22, 1985

School was so mega-boring, I almost had a nosebleed!

Youth Club was wicked. Me and Evs got chased over the roof by the caretaker. Totally bricked ourselves.

After Youth Club, we pretended to Bridget that Sharron (Kim's cousin) was having some with Dave on the side and Kim got really angry.

We put on a really ace act in the pub car park, but in the end we all cracked up and had to tell Bridget that it was fake. She didn't find it funny.

Good night.

I don't do a very good job of explaining this prank, and I'm not really sure what the purpose was. I suspect that Bridget had been caught spreading gossip and the other girls wanted to embarrass her.

Thursday, May 23, 1985

School was boring.

It's my sister's last day tomorrow and she is getting all upset about it. God knows why!

Dossed about in German as usual, and Miss has had to start locking the door before lesson, to stop us getting in there and writing obscenities on the blackboard.

After school, me, Benny, Evs, Fred and Marco played tennis and dossed about.

Apart from that today was just like any other day.

Boring.

Being a German lesson, the obscenities in question were usually about Hitler having only one testicle. I think one time there was a crude drawing of the teacher holding his scrotum and saying "yum".

Friday, May 24, 1985

Today in German we stuck blu-tack and chewing gum in the lock so that Miss couldn't get the key in to unlock the room. She had to go and fetch a spoon to try and poke it all out.

Today I acquired an exercise bike. Cool.

Me and Evs went to Benny's and we played on his computer.

'Sabre Wulf' on his BBC is just the same as on my Spectrum except better/worse sound in places.

Me and Evs were both later home. I didn't get bollocked though because I rang from Benny's phone and said I was running late before we left. Evs will probably get massacred though.

No Brass Band tomorrow. Yes!

Good night

Another entry which contains a surprise non-memory. To quote Obi-Wan Kenobi…I don't remember ever owning an exercise bike.

Benny had a BBC Micro, because, as previously mentioned – his Parents were quite well off.

Saturday, May 25, 1985

Stayed in bed and when everyone went out, I set up the exercise bike properly. It's ace now.

Me and Evs went into town this afternoon and I bought 'Your Spectrum' mag, plus a new lead for my tape recorder so I can copy games. That will be a great help.

I also bought the single of 'Parisienne Walkways' by Gary Moore. It's absolutely shit hot!

Paper Round tomorrow. Urghhh!

Went up to Benny's again with Evs, but I have left early today and gone straight to bed now, as my Dad says I can only have my pocket money if I get up by myself and don't rely on them having to drag me out of bed, screaming.

Night all.

Evs must have taken his tape recorder back, forcing me to upgrade my leads.

Clearly, after 3 months, my parents were tiring of having to wake me up every Sunday morning to do my Paper Round. This must have been the first time in my life that I was up before anyone else in the house.

Sunday, May 26, 1985

Paper Round this morning was excellent. Did my usual round for 65p, but then Pete asked me to do another full £1.30 round cos someone rang in sick. It took me 2 and half hours, but it earned me £2 in total so it was worth it.

Played on my computer nearly all day. Listened to my Gary Moore single and did a few miles on the exercise bike.

I'm a bit in love with Apollonia from 'Purple Rain' these days. I want to watch it again. Especially the bit by the lake!

There is the big Field Day on the park tomorrow. If the weather is good then it should be dead neat!

Good night.

"The bit by the lake". I think you can guess why.

The Field Day was an annual fund-raiser run by the local Cricket team. Mainly an excuse for everyone to get drunk on a Bank Holiday. They were always great fun, as long as it didn't rain.

Monday, May 27, 1985

The most boring Field Day ever took place today.

It rained all day. It had no high points and was mind-numbingly crap.

I just got absolutely caked in mud.

Everyone else has gone to the disco but I decided to stay in. I watched 'Alligator' on TV, it was pretty good.

Time: 12:14am. Way past my bedtime.

Good night.

Another film I have no memory of.

Tuesday, May 28, 1985

Totally boring.

Went to Evs, we walked aimlessly around the estate and eventually ended up back at his playing on his computer. I came home and did fuck all else today.

This is what school half-term holidays were like. There was just NOTHING to do.

Wednesday, May 29, 1985

Mum was at work today.

Evs couldn't come out so I was just on my own, playing on the computer all day.

I worked out how to do the loading screen for 'Cornelius The Worm' amongst other things.

Apart from that it was boring.

Steve rang me to see what I was doing, but he's a bit boring sometimes.

Progress on the game then. The loading screen…wow! I think I cooled on the whole idea after this, as Steve took it far too seriously.

Thursday, May 30, 1985

Went up to Nanna's today. Me and my Sister were bored so we went swimming at the pool near their house. As always my nose is now starting to get blocked up.

Went to Wilko's this morning to get some slug pellets for Nanna.

Also got a C12 data tape from WH Smith.

'The Rocky Horror Picture Show' is the only thing worth waiting for tomorrow. Today was sooooo BORING.

Something about Swimming Pools back then was the industrial levels of chlorine they would put in the water. It always wrecked my sinuses.

Friday, May 31, 1985

Stayed in Evs tent again in his garden. We trailed the TV into the tent and watched 'Rocky Horror'. It was right ace.

Lee Aaron was on E.C.T. and she was dead fit.

About 3am we snuck out for another night time wander around the estate. There is a girl in the year above who really fancies Evs so we walked down to her house. They had some washing out and Evs grabbed a pair of pants off the line. As we walked home I asked him why he did that and he said he didn't really know. I pointed out that they might be her mum's pants and his face was a picture. He then just chucked then in a bush.

Didn't sleep until 5:30 and then we woke up at 9:30. Only four hours sleep so I'm knackered now.

I'd never seen 'The Rocky Horror Picture Show' so I don't know why my expectations were so high. I remember being underwhelmed, but clearly not if I recorded it as "right ace".

E.C.T (Extra Celestial Transmission) was a short-lived Channel 4 show dedicated to Heavy Metal music. This was almost certainly the first time I'd heard Lee Aaron's music, and telling that I pass no comment on her artistry.

Saturday, June 1, 1985

Had a shower this morning when I got in.

Went to town but didn't buy anything.

Paper Round tomorrow, but I'm knackered so going to bed early tonight.

Dad has a new car, but he measured it wrong and it's too long to fit in in the garage. Ha!

The famous "Day that Dad bought a car which was too big to fit in the garage" is unforgettable to me. Unwittingly, this may be one of the greatest lessons he ever taught me.

Sunday, June 2, 1985

Got up OK for my Paper Round.

Spent all day on the computer and finished designing and doing the code for the loading screen on 'Cornelius'.

Steve better like it!

Watched a bit of 'That's Life' on TV. School tomorrow.

Ugh.

Better go to bed now then eh?

After all that, it goes unrecorded as to what Steve thought of my loading screen. The game, and our brief venture as a Software House is never mentioned again.

Monday, June 3, 1985

School was wank. Did bugger all.

Kerrang came and it has Lee Aaron in it again. Apparently she once did a topless shoot in some French magazine called 'Oui'. Cor!

Played tennis tonight with the lads. Phil reckons that his Dad gets Camera Weekly and there is a totally nude picture of Sam Fox in this week's issue! Not sure if that is true or not.

Night all.

You will not be surprised to learn that I never saw a copy of this French magazine. Perhaps I would be more lucky with Phil's Dad's copy of Camera Weekly?

Tuesday, June 4, 1985

School was once again, very boring. Went to my Cornet lesson, also went to Brass Band and Scouts tonight.

All very crap.

Watched 'Miami Vice' on TV when I got home.

Went to bed.

This was the first series of 'Miami Vice' and it was a really popular show, due to the music and fashion being so modern. I don't think I ever really understood where Miami was or what the "Vice Squad" did. I just knew it had loads of drugs and prostitutes in it. We all pretty much dressed like Don Johnson in the summer of 1985. All pastel colours and (knock-off) Ray-Ban Wayfarers.

Wednesday, June 5, 1985

What a surprise, Phil was bulling yet again about Camera Weekly!

Went to have my private lesson at Sam's house and Mum crashed the car into a wall.

School was crap.

I love Samanthan Fox.

I'm fairly sure that not a single thing Phil claimed, ever turned out to be true.

You will be pleased to know that this is the last mention of Samantha Fox.

Thursday, June 6, 1985

It rained all bloody day today.

Dead boring.

Went to Brass Band practice. Very boring.

But at least it meant I could skive from French.

Did fuck all else.

When there was a school concert in the offing, it meant that we were excused certain lessons to go and rehearse in the assembly hall.

Friday, June 7, 1985

Me and Evs went up to Benny's house tonight. Played on his computer and listened to his Billy Idol album on cassette. It is great.

I've left my coat at school so I have got to avoid needing to wear it because I'll get bollocked by Mum and Dad.

Dossed about some more in German. We played chair dominos.

Nite all!

Billy Idol's first LP began to act as a gateway towards more alternative music. His pop-rock stylings led me to his punk origins in Generation X, and onwards into all manner of classic punk, like the Sex Pistols, The Buzzcocks, then The Ramones and so on.

Chair Dominos is exactly as you'd imagine. Lining up chairs so that when you knock one over, they all go.

Saturday, June 8, 1985

Although the heading was written out, there was no entry for today. And there ended my solid run of writing a daily diary entry. A streak of 157 days. Things become more patchy from here on in, and I don't write again for 6 months.

Friday, December 13, 1985

Friday the 13th!

Probably the most important day of my life so far. In 15 minutes I depart to Benny's house. Evs never comes round any more. He is a twat. Benny is my new best mate

The reason is that we are all going to Debbie's party. Jacqui wants to get off with me and I know that I will. It's going to happen. I am shitting myself. Goodbye cruel world!

Quite what happened to end the friendship I had with Evs goes unrecorded. I don't remember any great bust-up, and calling him "a twat" seems harsh and unwarranted I guess we just drifted apart after the summer holidays, and because we'd chosen different 'O' Level subjects we were no longer in many classes together.

This particular diary entry was obviously prompted in anticipation of me getting my "first girlfriend". I don't write again for another 10 months.

Thursday, October 23, 1986

Well it really happened! I got off with Jacqui. Nobody really said anything at school the next day and it was a bit weird, but then a few days later it was my birthday and all the lads (me, Benny, Dave and Fred) had a bit of video party. We watched 'National Lampoon's Class Reunion'. It wasn't bad. Then I admitted under questioning that I did actually like her. So on the day we broke up from school for Christmas, she came round to my house with Debbie and the lads. We watched 'Every Which Way But Loose' on tele. Everyone left afterwards apart from Jacqui and we got off with each other again. We then went out officially for two whole weeks before I dumped her on Sunday 5th January (the day before we went back to school). I think that was one of the reasons I dumped her. I didn't want to have to be one of those lads who spends break times with his "girlfriend" rather than playing football. I didn't really pre-plan it but me and Benny were watching football on tele when she turned up at my house without warning. She had got quite clingy and possessive and it was getting on my tits. The more annoyed with her I got, the more clingy she was. It was good while it lasted, and it gave me valuable experience, plus a bit more confidence, but I've not been out with anyone since. Because I'm repulsive to most I guess (aaaah!) Since then I've been totally obsessing over Tara, but I know that's never going to happen as she is way out of my league. This last week I have been more interested in Ruth, a girl in the year below who is insanely fit but sadly taken. Back of the queue for me.

In the summer I went on a Brass Band tour to Holland. Me and one of the other band members called John met these two Dutch girls called Yvonne and Miriam. I paired off with

Yvonne, but there wasn't much we could do as I couldn't take her back to a shared dormitory! She was the last girl I kissed and fooled around with, but I'm working on it.

On Monday I bought Billy Idol's new album 'Whiplash Smile' which I have waited two years for! It's ace, Because I got it on the first day it came with a free poster. His latest single 'To Be A Lover' was on Top Of The Pops earlier tonight and the video was very funny. Right now, the repeat of 'Annika' is on TV. It's a rude Swedish drama. I've been going to the football quite a lot too. We got promoted last season which was great, but we've been pretty average this season. It's my 'O' Levels year now so naturally I have good stock of bog paper ready. Shitting it.

Fred's going out with my ex-love Louise. I don't care though as I gave up on her a long time ago. That's about the whole story. That's all you missed.

Quite the update. Probably the longest diary entry in the first two volumes. A lot had happened and it's evident that some 'growing-up' had occurred.

Incidentally, on the Dutch trip, one of the Tuba players lent me a tape of Jean-Michel Jarre's Oxygene & Equinoxe albums. These became the soundtrack of my 'O'-Level revision and even now if I have to concentrate on a piece of work for any length of time, I still put these on. It's so much easier to focus with instrumental music. The Smiths 'Queen Is Dead' LP was also out that summer and featured heavily on all our Sony Walkmans. Quite funny that we were supposed to be concentrating on our JP Sousa marches, but instead were all knee-deep in sharing Morrissey's angst.

24 October 1986 STATS

Age: 15 years, 10 months

Weight: 9 stone 7 pounds

Height: 5 feet 8 inches

Foot: Size 8.5

Likes: Tara, Ruth, Billy Idol, Marillion, Alternative Comedy, Yorkshire Pudding

Dislikes: Smoking, Soul/Disco music, Albion Market

Favourite Film: The Supergrass

Favourite Car: Toyota MR2

Favourite Album: Billy Idol – Whiplash Smile

Favourite Book: 3 Men In A Boat – Jerome K Jerome

Thankfully my interest in sporty cars didn't last long, and I've never owned anything even remotely resembling a "good car". I blame Miami Vice.

'Albion Market' was a short-lived ITV soap opera, like a crap cousin to 'Coronation Street'.

One of my Sister's boyfriends got me into Marillion and it signified my interest in more cerebral music, although I'd never heard early Genesis so I wasn't to know they weren't quite as ground-breaking as I perhaps thought they were.

Friday, October 24, 1986

Tonight I have watched nil TV. I have however done the following things.

1) Mended my shelf
2) Listened to the Billy Idol album
3) Made myself a cheese and chive muffin
4) Had a glass of McEwan's Export
5) Made myself some toast (which I burnt!)
6) Taped The Housemartins' album "London 0 – Hull 4" which Jimbo lent me today at school. It is pretty decent.

We broke up for half-term today and next Thursday Benny and scouse Nikki are having a joint party. I'm looking forward to it, but I'm not sure who is going, and who I might try and get off with. Jayne may be there, so we shall see. She just broke up with her boyfriend today, which may be good news if I play my cards right! Ringing Benny in the morning to see if he knows who is going. Can't afford to go the footy today, as I already bought a ticket for next Wednesday's game instead. They better win. Seems like they always do when I don't go. Enough for today. Nothing else to relate.

Genuinely surprised to see my Parents letting me drink alcohol around the house at 15! That Housemartins LP was another game-changer.

Tuesday, November 4, 1986

Today was our second day back at school after the half-term holiday. Benny & Nikki's party was really shit. Jayne didn't go, but worse than that, there were no single girls there at all, except for one, but we hate each other so that was never going to happen. I got quite drunk and went to sleep half way through it. Went to my Grandma's 80th birthday party and it was alright. Dad actually bought me a vodka and lime!

Today I see the very fit Tara has had her haircut and it makes her look even fitter than ever. The business with Ruth has hotted up as well as yesterday she told Martyn that she did fancy me but she already has a boyfriend. So I just have to wait. Today she kept looking at me in a way that could be interpreted as "longingly". Or maybe she just didn't have her glasses on? I think she is easily on a par with Tara, but I think it's more likely to ever happen with her rather than Tara because she is in the year below, and it's cool to be seen going out with older lads. Tara know I fancy her but she is not interested. I think she may also have an older boyfriend. She just ignores me whenever I see her.

Of course we won the football when I didn't go, and drew on Wednesday night when I did. Typical. I went with Fred and Dave and it was a good laugh anyway. I have Brass Band practice now so got to go!

And then buying me alcohol in Public House? That's illegal!

Monday, November 10, 1986

I didn't go the game at the weekend and we won yet again!

On to the subject of girls. Aaaah! I'm a tortured soul and Tara is the least of my problems. On Friday before the school's Autumn Fayre, Ruth rang me! I totally shat my pants when I realised who it was. She wanted to know if Dave was going out with anyone. I had to disappoint her obviously because he very much is, but she wouldn't tell me who wanted to know. She was very quick to re-assure me that it wasn't her, so that was a relief. I think it was either her friend Nicky or her sister Sandra. If it was Nicky then the call was totally unnecessary as she knows full well that Dave has a girlfriend. In which case it could just have been an excuse to ring and talk to me, but I doubt it because she just ignores me at school. I spoke to her sister a few times but not about Ruth. These things just prey on my mind at night and it all drives me mad. Why is nothing ever simple? I wish someone could just put me out of my misery.

I made a hi-hat out of loads of bits of drumkit that I stole from school and from band practice. I don't know why as it's useless without the rest of the drumkit. And it's no replacement for a girlfriend. As for my hopes that I may stand a chance with Ruth over Tara because she is younger, I heard today on the grapevine that Ruth's boyfriend is 23 years old! God help me.

What possessed me to steal stuff to make a hi-hat I'll never know.

Tuesday, November 11, 1986

Here I am writing 2 days on the trot. Just like old times eh?

I was ignored by Ruth again all day today. I'm beginning to accept that I will never go out with her, especially as she is taken, but even if she ever becomes single again. I just can't see it. But I have patience.

We saw her last week sitting in Physics on a Wednesday periods 5& 6 so today we sat there and wrote messages to her on the desk in the hope that she will see them tomorrow.

I borrowed "The Seer" album by Big Country off Plonky. It's OK I suppose as background music. I lent him my Billy Bragg records.

Plonky lent me so many great records, as he had older brothers who were into really good stuff. I remember him bringing round all of the Elvis Costello albums and loads of New Order 12"s but I don't recall borrowing this particular Big Country LP. It's definitely not their best (I don't think they ever beat 'The Crossing'), so most likely I forgot because I didn't choose to tape it.

Wednesday, November 19, 1986

Wicked! Boy oh boy has a lot happened today!

First, Ruth said 'Hello' to me at school!

Second, I have been invited to a party that some girl in the year below is having! 21st December. No idea why – but I'm hoping it's because Ruth asked her to invite me.

Third, I found out that Jacqui still wants to go out with me and asked if we could get back together. Help!

Rachel C is also having a party on Saturday 20th December at her house. Two parties in two days. Will I survive? Bearing in mind that on the Sunday morning I have to get up and do my Paper Round. Aah – I do not look forward to that bit.

Went to the football again and we won 1-0. Going again to the next game with my cousin John.

I scored in football in PE today. Watch out Gary Lineker!

Bought the cassette single of 'Ask' by The Smiths.

Got a Cornet lesson tonight. Boo!

I seem to be writing more frequently, albeit sporadically and in line with whatever excitement is happening on the (potential) relationship front. Or maybe it was the novelty of scoring a goal in PE. I don't actually ever remember scoring a goal, but I guess I must have. I was useless at football.

Thursday, November 27, 1986

Had a wicked traumatic experience this afternoon after school. My sister slammed the glass porch door into my shoulder and it smashed. Glass everywhere. I have a huge cut on my shoulder and I had to go to the hospital. They gave me 6 stitches in it. Also had to have a tetanus injection in my arse. It's now dead sore when I sit down. I get the stitches out next Thursday. Long weekend Friday and Monday now.

I'm going to town in the morning with Kim. I might be going to the next away game with Di and her Dad too, waiting to find out if I can get a ticket.

Much pain! See ya

The trauma of this day still lives with me, as do the scars. There was blood everywhere and my Mum was hysterical. Looking back she was probably justified, as I was about 3 inches away from having my jugular sliced. I should add that it wasn't a malicious act on behalf of my sister. We had just been racing to get the post. I beat her to it and she tried to shut me in the porch by closing the door behind me. Unbeknownst to her, I had turned around and was already heading back into the hallway when SMASH!

Monday, December 15, 1986

Tomorrow is my 16th Birthday. How exciting? Over the past weekend there have been two parties. Last Friday was the Cricket & Football club do – at the Golf Club. This was OK. My Dad was buying me drinks. I had 3 pints of Bitter, 2 Vodka and Limes and 1 Lager & Black. I was very merry and had no hangover! My Dad did.

I bought a new outfit (jacket & shoes) for the party last night. It was Helen A's birthday. Her parents run a hotel so the party was there. Because it's their place, they wouldn't serve any of us drinks, so me and Dave walked to the Off-License round the corner. Dave looks older than me so he went in and got the drinks. Like a twat he bought me a litre of Cider. Big mistake. I drank it really quickly. Someone else had smuggled some beer and vodka into the party, so I then had a can of Schlitz beer, more cider and a swig of vodka from the bottle. Next thing I knew I was very drunk and being hideously sick. Typical me. First time I get sick on booze and it has to be that party. Ruth was there and she was asking for me. They had to tell her I was puking in the Gents. What a twat I am.

I also found out that one of Ruth's mates called Nicky is also interested in me. She's really nice so I might try and get to know her and see if it works out. She will be at the party next week, so we shall see. I'm working on the assumption that Ruth isn't going to dump her fella for me. I'm still so mad about getting sick last night (he goes on…)

Didn't go to the away game as planned because Di decided she didn't want to go. We lost anyway. Still near the top of the table though.

Next Saturday is Rachel C's party and Jacqui will be there. God help me. I'm such a twat.

From here on in it's largely drinking and girls, so if your primary interest is in ZX Spectrum chat (or you are aggrieved that the Samanthan Fox story arc never achieved satisfactory denouement), then you may want to step away.

Wednesday, December 24, 1986

Two parties last weekend which I must tell you about.

First Rachel C's party on the Saturday. Jacqui got really pissed out of her head and kept putting her arms around me, crying, and telling me that she loved me. It got really embarrassing after a bit. She then got off with Benny just to try and make me jealous. Benny was pretty pissed too, so he just went along with it. I didn't really care. I could have taken advantage of her in that state, but I just felt sorry for her. She was saying she'd do anything I wanted her to. Funny how you dream about stuff like that — then when it happens it's the least sexy thing ever.

Second, Sarah W's 4th Year party on the Sunday. Me, Plonky and Dave all got invited and went to this one. Nicky was there and made it clear that she wanted to get off with me. I talked to her for a bit and she was really nice, but then I got dead scared and avoided her for about an hour. This made her upset and Ruth and her friends started to call me a twat for leading her on. I had no idea what to do, so I had a pint and then went to apologise to her. Next thing I know it's the end of the night and they are playing The Housemartins' 'Caravan Of Love' so I kissed her. I was shaking with nerves, but it was great. Me, Plonky and Dave walked all the way home and I didn't get back until 1:30am.

I hoped that Nicky might ring me, but she hasn't. I'd ring her but I don't have her number and there are 5 people in the phone book with the same surname as her. I should be able to get it from someone else if I ask around enough. I'll try that and then ring her at the weekend, once Christmas is over. I'm not sure if I should start going out with her or not as we have our mock

'O' Levels in January. I really would like to though.

The Brass Band played Christmas Carols at the side of the pitch at half time of the football last Sunday and we won. Ace!

Look at me, wondering whether to prioritise my exams over a girlfriend. Such a swot. In reality I was probably just looking for excuses to avoid being brave and asking her out.

Thursday, January 15, 1987

Such a lot has happened since the New Year, and it is brilliant!

On New Year's Eve, Me, Benny and Jim had a get-together at my house. Benny had to leave at 11 so me and Jim saw the new year in, watching Whistle Test. The Smiths were on doing 'Big Mouth'

I rang up Nicky to say happy new year, but she was out at a party. I ended up talking to her mum for ages. I was pretty drunk but her mum seemed lovely!

Nicky didn't ring me back though so I was sad

Me and Jim played snooker at a club in town during the school holidays and he introduced me to a new dish at the chip shop, called a Doner Kebab. Pretty tasty!

Back at school and Nicky apologized for not ringing me back. We didn't speak much over the next few days on account of me being such a coward and worrying that she had lost interest. Eventually I decided that I needed to get a bit brave and just see what happened. I had nothing to lose. Things were just starting to get going when splat! She went on her School trip for a week, so we've been leading a telephone conversation romance. I rang her last Saturday morning but she was just leaving for work, so she rang me back in the evening. We were on the phone for over an hour! Anyone who can keep me on the phone for that long must be worth something

Anyway on the Monday she was back at school and we talked for all of Dinner hour, and then she left for the trip. I was dead upset. She's still there now but she has rung me every night.

Twice tonight in fact! I'm definitely going to ask her out properly when she gets back. This should be Friday night, but it's snowed really heavy everywhere and they may be stranded up in the hills. I hope she makes it back OK.

I've got my mocks this week and next week. I think I'd be suicidal if it wasn't for Nicky. I can't wait to see her again!

I thought Nicky's Mum was great, and she used to talk to me loads, in a way that my friends' mums never did. She was quite a lot younger than my Mum, and doing the maths, I'm sure that she must have been in her mid-thirties. It's only now that I realise she was almost certainly engaging in some mild, vicarious flirting with me on the phone.

But more importantly this was "My First Doner Kebab Day".

15 January 1987 STATS

Age: 16 years, 1 month

Weight: 10 stone

Height: 5 feet 8 inches

Foot: Size 9

Likes: Nicky, Billy Idol, Billy Bragg, Marillion, The Smiths, The Housemartins, Filthy, Rich & Catflap, Yorkshire Pudding

Dislikes: Smoking, Soul/Disco music

Favourite Film: The Supergrass or Coast To Coast

Favourite Car: Toyota MR2

Favourite Album: Billy Bragg – Talking With The Taxman About Poetry

Favourite Book: Adrian Mole Diaries

'Coast to Coast' was a comedy road-movie starring Lenny Henry that featured loads of old soul songs. I remember it being amazing, but apparently it's never been reshown because they had problems licensing all the music. 'Filthy, Rich & Catflap' was the follow-up to 'The Young Ones' which we all desperately wanted to love, but dare not admit that it wasn't anywhere near as good.

Sunday, June 28, 1987

I'm at my most relaxed than I have been for ages. No more exams, no girl trouble, just doing what I want in life. Since I last wrote, I went out with Nicky for a couple of months and it was going well, but then she packed me in for no reason. Then she asked me back out again, and we were back on for a while . Then I packed her in.

I really like Hannah, I mean REALLY like her, but she's almost my best mate. I tried to explain this to her at the Leavers Party, but she was quite drunk and I don't think she really understood what I was trying to say. I don't care how my 'O' Levels turn out at the moment. Just give me a job. Give me something to do and I'm away. Doing nothing makes you realise how important it is to have money in your pocket. I doubt that I will write again unless anything significant happens. That may be a long time!

Another 5 month gap between entries, which I guess can be explained by that being the stressful time of revising for and sitting 'O' Levels. This entry comes shortly after my last exam

I finally admit my feelings for Hannah too. We sat together in 'O' Level biology class for two years, so it had been brewing a while. Painfully unrequited of course!

28 June 1987 STATS

Age: 16 years, 7 months

Weight: 10 stone

Height: 5 feet 8 inches

Foot: Size 9

Likes: Hannah, Billy Bragg, Elvis Costello, The Smiths, Black Adder II, Yorkshire Pudding

Dislikes: Smoking, Problems with girls/love-life, exams

Favourite DJ: John Peel

Favourite Film: Blade Runner

Favourite Car: Anything that goes

Favourite Album: Lloyd Cole - Rattlesnakes

Favourite Book: Back To Basics With Billy Bragg

By this point there was no Heavy Metal, or Prog Rock on the agenda. It was pure Indie. My sister got me into The Smiths and I never looked back.

Monday, February 8, 1988

Well, it really is difficult to believe how my life can be so utterly depressing. I seem to get shitted on in love, time and time again. I nearly went back out with Nicky again, but then she got off with Kenny just to make me jealous at a party. This was 2 days after we had agreed to go out again. (it was October last year I think). I don't have time for that sort of messing around, so I vowed to never kiss her again. So far I have managed that OK although I had to put up strong resistance a couple of times.

I had a brief fling with one of her friends – Frances. It only happened once, but then she also went and got off with Kenny the next time I saw her. He's a right bastard. So plopped on there too.

I decided not to go to Sixth Form as I am sick of all the same faces I grew up with. Nothing ever changes. I ended up at College instead doing a BTEC in Business Studies. I hate it sooo much.

The people at College are even more small-minded and immature. It really gets me down, so I've started to skive off a bit. The bus to College goes past the train station so some days I just get off and hop on a train and wander around places where no one knows me.

Last week I went to Birmingham. This week I think I will go to Leicester. We are probably moving to Scotland anyway because of Dad's job.

Love, work and life in general get me down so much and parents don't understand. I sometimes feel morbidly obsessed with death but I'm normal really. Honest!

College itself is good. So many fit girls in general but they aren't in my classes so what do I do? Problems, problems…

A 7 month gap between the previous entry and this update, so no record of the school Summer Holiday or my first term at Sixth Form College.

I don't even mention my 'O'-Level results (I passed everything – just. I only got one A and that was in Biology).

I'm not sure what happened to trigger a resumption of the diary, but between here and the end of Volume 2, I write most days. We never did move to Scotland, but it must have been a real possibility for me to mention it here. My Dad worked in a factory and this was just as Thatcher was busy gutting the country. He seemed to be permanently facing redundancy wherever he moved to.

8 February 1988 STATS

Age: 17 years, 1 month

Weight: 10 stone 12lbs

Height: 5 feet 8 and a half inches

Likes: Hannah, The Wedding Present, Billy Bragg, Joy Division/New Order, The Smiths (RIP), laughter in general, Good Old Yorkshire Pudding

Dislikes: Small-minded people with pathetic attitudes, the Beastie Boys and crap pop music

Favourite DJ: The one and only John Peel

Favourite Film: Roxanne (gives you hope)

Favourite Car: Touchy subject

Favourite Album: The Wedding Present – George Best

Favourite Book: 3 Men In A Boat – Jerome K Jerome (still makes me laugh)

Beautiful that through it all, my one constant love affair has been with the Yorkshire Pudding. Steve Martin's 'Roxanne' was a big favourite of Plonky's, as he was also blessed with a larger than average nose.

Tuesday, February 9, 1988

Today was absolutely crap at College. Everyone really pissed me off, and then when the day finished I hung around for a bit and ended up having a down to earth chat with this guy Stephen on my course who is usually a bit of a Tory twat, but he was being nice to me. This meant I got a later bus home and I saw Anthony that used to go to my school. He's the one that got me into The Beatles and taught me some stuff on guitar. Had a good chat with him too. Then I saw Benny when he got on the bus in town. He passed his driving test yesterday. He said he would take me out for a drive sometime.

John Peel played the new Wedding Present single (ace) and their contribution to the NME compilation tape Sgt Pepper Knew My Father ('Getting Better') – also ace. Then he played Morrissey's debut solo single! Today started off so crap but gradually became a good day. I go to sleep happy for once. Going to Leicester tomorrow

---

The Sixth-Form College was the other side of town to the suburb where I grew up, and it was huge compared to my old school. It would be fair to say that I had led a fairly insular life in terms of social class. Our suburb was fully Middle-Class and there were no more than a handful of non-white kids in the school. College on the other hand was a complete cross-section of the areas class and ethnicity. An eye-opener for sure, and no real surprise that it took me a long time to settle in.

Wednesday, February 10, 1988

Went to Leicester to do a bit of shopping. I bought The Smiths 'Girlfriend In A Coma' 12" for 99p, 1000 Violins 'If I Were A Bullett..' 12" for £2 and the first The The 7" 'Controversial Subject' on blue vinyl for £6. It's not very good but it is rare so I can probably sell it on for loads.

No College tomorrow I don't think, so I will stop in and just listen to records. I'll have to see Plonky before tomorrow night as there is a party and I need a ticket. Baking also tomorrow.

Today was so relaxing. This is what not having to face twats at College does for you!

11:30pm Listening to John Peel as always but not long until I will be dancing to The Wedding Present live as me and Simon are going on the train to see them at Trent Poly.

Over 17 years on this earth, 7 'O' Levels to my name and only one really meaningful girlfriend. Will I ever be happy? I doubt it but I hope so.

That 'The The' single turned out to be a bootleg and not an original so I didn't get much for it.

Thursday, February 11, 1988

Skived off College again on some piss poor excuse, but Mum believed me. It might have been valid. I'm not too sure. I doubt it.

Scrubbed the Bakery, and then after that went to a party in town. It was shit. We danced to The Smiths and I had a nice talk with Hannah. I really put my foot in it sometime but I really do truly love her. When she laughs I go all funny inside. I feel sorry for her though because she is obsessed with John A (and Dave before him) – and they have both been total bastards to her. Getting off with her and then blanking her. They hurt her as much as she hurts me. Why can't she see that I'd be hers forever if she'd let me be her boyfriend?

My Grandma gave me a condom today. It came free with her magazine she said. It has an expiry date on it of 1992, so will probably be long out of date before I ever get to use it.

Might actually go to College tomorrow and face the twats. Everyone else seemed to be having a good time tonight. When will I be happy?

I seemed to be embracing the fact that educational attendance was no longer mandatory. I'd also started my first proper job, working Saturdays and Wednesday evenings in the local Sainsburys Bakery. It mainly entailed cleaning up the mess, but I did it for 2 years (and then occasional shifts after that) so I did get to learn some baking skills eventually.

Saturday, February 13, 1988

Today has been a good day. I got up this morning to go to work, and I got the mail. There was a massive letter for me. At first I thought it was a Valentines Day card, but on closer examination, the address on the envelope was in my writing (on an S.A.E) and it was postmarked LEEDS! Weeks ago I had sent off for The Wedding Present's newsletter and this was the reply. As well as the newsletter I got a handwritten thank you note in cool-brown ink from David Gedge! Work in the Bakery was a real comedown after that, but now I'm just looking forward to the gig even more.

S.A.E being a stamped-addressed envelope – which was what you had to include in any correspondence if you wanted to receive a reply.

Sunday, February 14, 1988

Valentine's Day here again. Surprise surprise! No cards for me, but then I didn't send any so what is there to worry about? Got up at 12:30pm for dinner and argued with Mum and Dad all day. Read my Wedding Present newsletter again. Not much cracking off at College tomorrow. Everyone else is off doing Work Experience so I will have nothing to do all day. Morrissey's first solo single is out tomorrow. I will be snapping up a copy for sure. Might go round to see if Plonky is in.

Nicky rang me on both Friday and Saturday nights when I was out and I was supposed to call her back this morning, but as I didn't wake up until the afternoon, that was impossible. She is probably pissed off with me. Never mind. More tomorrow

---

Plonky lived a good 20 minute walk from my house, so this was no small endeavour to undertake on the off-chance that he was in.

Monday, February 15, 1988

Got to College this morning and was simply told to "get on with something in the library". I thought – sod that – and came straight back home again. Stupid work experience! Stopped off in town to change buses and went in Virgin where I saw the Joy Division video for £10 so I bought that, and then went round to Plonky's. Hannah and Ellen also came round. I asked Hannah if she got any Valentine's Day cards and she said no. This really surprised me a lot. Good job I never sent her one. It would have been so obvious!

Plonky wanted to change his Cure video that he bought but the tape broke, so I gave him some cash to get the Morrissey single. He brought the goods round about 7pm. We listened to it and had a good chat. I played my guitar (one true love) and we watched Brookside, Red Dwarf (not bad) and Moonlighting (this was a good one). After the latter, he went home and I went to bed.

Oh Nicky rang again, but I was a bit abrupt with her as I was in the middle of talking to Plonky. Wedding Present gig coming up – can't wait. This boy can't wait.

My electric guitar was a Hondo semi-acoustic (a cheap Gibson 335 copy). Amazingly this was the first ever episode of Red Dwarf, and it went on to be a real favourite of mine. It got much better as the characters developed.

The Joy Division video was such bad quality that I thought it was faulty, but no, it was just like that.

Tuesday, February 16, 1988

Came straight back from College again and stopped in all day writing songs on guitar and playing records. Sgt. Pepper NME tape came this morning. It's very good, especially The Wedding Present, Billy Bragg, The Fall and Michelle Shocked tracks. Wrote 2 songs today. One is about seeing these two central characters arguing in public, and thinking how silly they look and then remembering that we all do that sometimes. The other one is about a 4 year old boy not having the slightest idea what is going to happen to him when he grows up.

I have no memory or written/recorded evidence of either of these songs, so if I wrote the words down then I must have binned them at a later date. From the description they sound crap anyway.

Wednesday, February 17, 1988

What a great day – went to The Wedding Present gig. Bought a t-shirt with balloons on it and then the support band came on. It was The Flatmates, they were really good and encored with 'Every Day' by Buddy Holly. Then The Wedding Present came on and did 12 songs before going off and then coming back on to do 2 more for their encore. They did 'Happy Birthday' by Altered Images and 'This Boy Can Wait' . Then they came back out again and did a second encore which was a crazy fast cover of 'It's Not Unusual' by Tom Jones!

Afterwards me and Simon hung around outside the back door as our train wasn't for a while so we had time to kill. There was a Leeds minivan near the back door and soon enough the band came out and started loading gear into it. We chatted to them for a while to pass the time. Nice blokes!

Then we went off to get the train and came home really happy!!

Long-time fans of The Wedding Present might be amused at my description of a double-encore, as not long after this tour the band stopped doing encores altogether.

Thursday, February 18, 1988

Nothing much happened today. I went to my Electives lesson, which is just some stupid doss thing where you can do what you like. We're doing a College magazine so I wrote a review of last night's gig. Came home and played my guitar and then went to work in the bakery (yawn).

I still have a copy of the College magazine and my review is not only, almost identical to the diary entry on the previous page, but also a complete outlier in terms of the rest of the magazine's contents. Everyone else was writing articles about the food in the canteen, the state of the toilets, and how to deal with exam stress etc etc. The only other piece in the "Entertainments" section was the song lyrics to Debbie Gibson's "Shake Your Love", contributed by a shy gay kid who sat in the corner and tried not to talk to anyone and seemed constantly petrified of everyone and everything. Memories like that really bring it home how tough it must have been to be non-hetero-normative back then.

Sunday, February 21, 1988

First day of work experience tomorrow. Total shit or what? Did sod all today. Worked all day yesterday at Sainsburys. It was stock taking so I had to do a 12 hour shift from 8:15am to 8:15pm.

I did however go out in my dinner break to the Record Fair in town where I bought a Smiths bootleg tape of some demos, a Billy Bragg live bootleg and a Lloyd Cole bootleg which I am going to give Plonky. The Billy Bragg tape is great, there are 3 unreleased new songs on there. His new album should be great if this is anything to go by. The Wedding Present new single is out tomorrow, so I'll buy that too. Going to sleep now listening to 'Waiting For The Great Leap Forwards' by Billy Bragg. Night.

Stock taking was always the worst day A total slog. It didn't help that I had no idea what I was doing or why. Record Fairs back then would just have table after table of audience-recorded bootleg live tapes. A real goldmine of stuff – and a total lottery when it came to audio quality.

Monday, February 22, 1988

First day of the Work Experience was totally shit, but I soon got used to it. Even now though I'm dreading tomorrow. Who wants to work in a bank?

Today was a bugger because I forget my money so I couldn't but The Wedding Present 12" as planned. I was so annoyed with myself.

Weird that I didn't mention where the Work Experience took place. It was in the Cooperative Bank in town and I hated every minute of it. Having done a Paper Round and then worked in a Bakery, I just couldn't believe how tedious it was to work in an office. No one really seemed to do anything, and what they did do made no sense to me. I made my mind up right there and then, that this wasn't the job for me. I think this is when I also started to regret taking Business Studies at College.

Saturday, February 27, 1988

Work Experience is over thank god. Never going to do that again. I did my back in on Thursday so rang in sick to Sainsburys. Worked today though. Finally bought The Wedding Present 12" and it's friggin' ace. Also they are on the front of Sounds, with an interview in Melody Maker and a gig review in NME. This morning I got a letter from some bloke offering Wedding Present live bootleg tapes (I sent off for it from an advert in Sounds). Morrissey's single went straight into the charts at number 6, Primitives single in at 29.

Now I'm preparing for the College trip to Germany next week (we leave on March 6th)

I don't remember hurting my back, so I could well have just been skiving to avoid work. The College trip to Germany on the other hand, I remember very well and it was a lot of fun. I finally managed to bond with a few people on my course, and I also met a German girl…but that's all in Volume III I'm afraid..

Tuesday, March 1, 1988

Yesterday was the leap year. 29th Feb. No one asked me to marry them. No surprise there.

I never asked anyone either, so sod it. Being back at College is crap. I don't really talk to many people, only Steve and Tall Ian – but I don't really like either of them. The thought of going to Germany with this lot is depressing. Someone help me.

And so ends Volume Two, where I very much did NOT write every day (something I hugely regret as there are a few things missing that I have strong memories of.)

No document of the Live Aid concert in July 1985 (which we recorded in its entirety on our brand new VHS player and re-watched repeatedly for months).

No document of our eventful family holiday to Corfu in June 1987 where I befriended three incredibly attractive girls from Stoke (and felt like king of the world). They were totally relaxed about sun bathing topless and so I had to play it cool, even though I was dying of embarrassment inside, and trying not to look.

No document of my first term at Sixth-Form College (which, as you can tell, was a massive shock to the system after leaving school).

No document of my first proper gig (The Cure Birmingham NEC 6th Dec-87.

And no document of my Parents buying me my first Electric Guitar as a reward for passing my 'O' Levels. Other than this beautifully drawn picture I did in the margins…

To Be Continued

ABOUT THE AUTHOR

Mark Highwater was born in small English midlands town towards the end of 1970. He is married with two children and a dog. He still lives close to where he grew up and both of his children attended the same school as the one he describes in these diaries. Boredom, it seems, suits him rather well.

This is his first book.

Printed in Great Britain
by Amazon